Improving Student Learning

ONE TEACHER at a TIME

SECOND EDITION

ASCD MEMBER BOOK

Many ASCD members received this book as a
member benefit upon its initial release.

Learn more at: **www.ascd.org/memberbooks**

Improving Student Learning

ONE TEACHER at a TIME

SECOND EDITION

Jane E. Pollock
Laura J. Tolone

 Alexandria, Virginia USA

1703 N. Beauregard St. • Alexandria, VA 22311-1714 USA
Phone: 800-933-2723 or 703-578-9600 • Fax: 703-575-5400
Website: www.ascd.org • E-mail: member@ascd.org
Author guidelines: www.ascd.org/write

Ranjit Sidhu, *CEO & Executive Director;* Stefani Roth, *Publisher;* Genny Ostertag, *Director, Content Acquisitions;* Julie Houtz, *Director, Book Editing & Production;* Megan Doyle, *Editor;* Thomas Lytle, *Creative Director;* Donald Ely, *Art Director;* Valerie Younkin, *Senior Production Designer;* Kelly Marshall, *Manager, Project Management;* Trinay Blake, *E-Publishing Specialist*

PAPERBACK ISBN: 978-1-4166-2969-6   ASCD product #117013

PDF E-BOOK ISBN: 978-1-4166-2970-2; see Books in Print for other formats.

Quantity discounts are available: e-mail programteam@ascd.org or call 800-933-2723, ext. 5773, or 703-575-5773. For desk copies, go to www.ascd.org/deskcopy.

ASCD Member Book No. FY21-3 (Dec. 2020 P). ASCD Member Books mail to Premium (P), Select (S), and Institutional Plus (I+) members on this schedule: Jan, PSI+, Feb, P; Apr, PSI+; May, P; Jul, PSI+; Aug, P; Sep, PSI+ Nov, PSI+; Dec, P. For current details on membership, see www.ascd.org/membership.

Library of Congress Cataloging-in-Publication Data
Names: Pollock, Jane E., 1958- author. | Tolone, Laura J., author.
Title: Improving student learning one teacher at a time / Jane E. Pollock, Laura J. Tolone.
Description: Second edition. | Alexandria, Virginia USA : ASCD, [2021] | Includes bibliographical references and index.
Identifiers: LCCN 2020033699 (print) | LCCN 2020033700 (ebook) | ISBN 9781416629696 (paperback) | ISBN 9781416629702 (pdf)
Subjects: LCSH: Effective teaching—United States. | Academic achievement—United States.
Classification: LCC LB1025.3 .P65 2021 (print) | LCC LB1025.3 (ebook) | DDC 371.102—dc23
LC record available at https://lccn.loc.gov/2020033699
LC ebook record available at https://lccn.loc.gov/2020033700

To my parents, Mary Ann and Bob Pollock

—JEP

With gratitude to Carol, Bill, and George for their
encouragement and support, and to Brien, Nate, Jen,
Najela, and Thairy for their mentorship and friendship

—LT

Improving Student Learning
ONE TEACHER at a TIME

SECOND EDITION

1. The Big Four... 1
    Teacher Voice: Gary Nunnally 16

2. Curriculum Design from Standards to Units to Daily Lessons 26
    Teacher Voice: Belinda Parini.....................................48

3. Lesson Planning, Delivery, and What the Students Do 51
    Teacher Voice: Jennifer Collins 76

4. Assessment Tasks 80
    Teacher Voices: McKinzie Sanders and Patrick Villareal 96

5. Feedback and Monitoring Student Progress Aligned
    to the Standards 101
    Teacher Voice: Ricky Sinfield.....................................112

Acknowledgments 117

Appendix: Thinking Skills Processes 118

References and Resources...124

Index 127

About the Authors 132

1
The Big Four

Gary Nunnally, a secondary social studies/history teacher in Nebraska, was participating in a staff development seminar on instructional strategies. Sitting in the back row with his leg in a cast, Gary appeared to be giving Jane, one of the authors of this book, the dismissive "talk to the hand" signal with the underside of his foot. It was fitting, given the heated exchange they were about to have about teaching, learning, and homework. Every time she would suggest how to use one of the research-based instructional strategies, Gary responded that he might try it if it would motivate the students to finish their homework. He said that he could only do so much in class, but students needed to take responsibility to complete all homework assignments to get good grades. At one point he argued that he could not even plan daily lessons because the following day relied on students completing homework. Gary noted that his students' disinterest in completing work was the cause of behavioral problems in his classroom, plummeting grades in his course, and, by extension, many uncomfortable parent–teacher conferences.

After his many interruptions, Jane asked Gary if he could possibly identify the number of students in each class who were not performing to the level that he expected—that would be a start in a positive direction. Without hesitating, Gary responded that there were four or five students he called "the disengagers" because they were attending but just did not participate fully in the class. He added that it meant that over the course of a day, 5 students per class added up to 25, or almost a class itself! When they opened the question to the other teachers from all grade levels in the session, it seemed that they, too, identified four or five students in every class who by their judgment should be performing better. Depending on the grade levels or subjects, teachers surmised reasons mostly related to factors outside of the classroom. Teachers agreed they wanted to find a way to improve learning with strategies that would help the four or five students in every class, but they stated their commitment to improving learning for all children. What was so impressive was that all of the teachers took personal responsibility; they described how they constantly tried harder to find new ways to help the students, *hoping* that those new ways would work, even if it was not a school or a district initiative. It seemed to us that they were initiating reforms one teacher at a time.

Gary offered that he wanted to take the "hope" out of his classroom. "I do not want to hope that the students will do well; I want to be able to plan for it to happen and be glad when I see the results for every student in my classes."

Replacing Hope with Certainty

"Take hope out of schools" would seem an unusual slogan for someone who wants to improve student learning. But, recall how many times you and your colleagues are likely to have said, "I *hope* this lab works; I spent a lot of time collecting the specimens and setting it up for my students." "I *hope* the students can identify the adverbs and adjectives on the test; I spent so much time reviewing." "I *hope* that tonight's concert goes well; I worked so hard and went over every piece again in today's rehearsal."

Over the years, one can see how schools take on improvement initiatives, specifically regarding structural reforms such as scheduling or student groupings, special programs, new technologies, and creative resources. All of them contribute enormously to improving the system but unfortunately fall short on the student achievement gains, as those do not seem to increase significantly. In this book, we share what we learned when we listened to individual teachers tell us what was working, but also what they were willing to slightly adjust when we shared new research. We focus on using research about teaching and learning to help teachers like Gary, who works really hard but gets frustrated with students who do not participate. It may also be helpful to new teachers who struggle to find efficient routines and ways to use time better in class.

To take hope out of school and replace it with certainty, we revisited the classic framework that guides teaching and learning: curriculum, instruction, and assessment. To our surprise, it appeared to be missing the one piece that can actually increase student performance.

The Missing Piece

Remember the diagram in the teaching text that showed the three points of a triangle labeled with the terms *curriculum, instruction,* and *assessment?* The lines were arrows indicating the interconnectedness of the three (see Figure 1.1). The promise of this framework was that teachers would teach and assess to the curriculum, creating the perfect feedback loop in which all students would learn.

FIGURE 1.1
The Curriculum-Instruction-Assessment Model

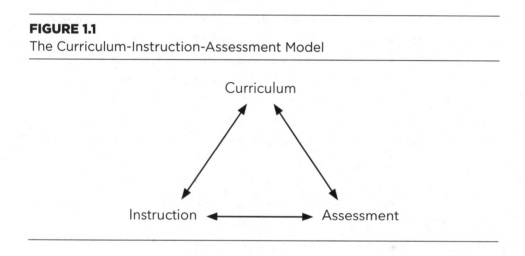

Listening to teachers like Gary Nunnally, we know that is not true for all students. We began with curriculum. Most teachers, Gary commented, say that curriculum documents are wordy and formatted in lengthy, boxy columns. Because they are difficult to read, they do not serve to guide instruction on a daily basis. He said that after perusing them at the beginning of the year, they sit on shelves collecting dust or hide away in digital files. Because of past experiences, many teachers have developed a "this too shall pass" mentality when new standards appear or new curriculum initiatives begin. What teachers want, he said, is curriculum documents reformatted for better accessibility, brevity, and readability. Can we make the documents in such a way that, instead of having a long multipage document, they could be in separate files because we now have access to shared document files?

As far as instruction, or planning lessons, Gary admitted that over the years he learned that he needed to plan for the student activities. Unit planners, he said, often offer standards with lists of *optional* instructional activities. If you looked at his planning, he would describe the task that the students would do that day or for homework and any possible assessment opportunities. After writing the lessons, he would go back to the list of standards and attach the ones that were relevant as the standards for that day; often there were as many as four or five that seemed to fit each day. With so many, it did not seem viable to track student progress back to the standards—the lesson, yes, but not individual progress. That means that there could be a gap in the curriculum-instruction-assessment feedback loop that might be contributing to the "missing piece."

For assessment, Gary committed to providing two review days to ensure that students would do better on the summative unit or quarterly tests. Did they? Some, he told us, but not all students did well even though he also provided comprehensive review sheets. Retesting? No time if he wanted to cover the curriculum. Quizzes? No time for them as there was already enough testing with state tests taking up so much time. The elementary teachers were less likely to give assessments, per se, as they felt they were assessing a lot of the time, just not writing it down. Sometimes they were asked to use standards-based report cards, but since they only specified a few standards, they did not really track progress daily.

To recap, teachers have curriculums, but because they are dense or use unfriendly formats, teachers tend to be able to teach without closely following them. Teachers often plan activities as their lesson planning; importantly, they often choose standards after planning, so they might not teach them explicitly. Most teachers tell us that they design their own assessments or build them online, and they would not assess what they do not find time to teach. That could mean that some standards in the curriculum may not be assessed in depth or possibly at all. Time is always an issue, and the perception that there is too much assessment anyway discourages many teachers from adding formative assessment. As a result of these three issues, few teachers tell us that they score student work to the standards identified by the curriculum—and that detail provided the missing link that led us to create the Big Four.

We hypothesized that teachers need

- Curriculum documents formatted in a way that helps them pace the standards and the unpacked objectives,
- A schema for lesson planning and delivery that describes what they would do as well as what the students should do to be more engaged with learning in class,
- More formative assessment with more open-ended response opportunities directly tied back to the standards, and
- Multiple methods to provide students with productive feedback about individual progress on the standards.

The intention of curriculum-instruction-assessment was a pathway that focused on the teacher and the teaching, but the framework was inadvertently missing an explicit feedback loop that would directly connect the learner to the learning goals. The Big Four is a framework that intends to link student performance directly to the curriculum, instruction, and assessment; the update includes a fourth component that we refer to as "feedback to the standards."

The Big Four

The Big Four keeps what works in the curriculum-instruction-assessment model but shifts the focus toward providing feedback to the students about their progress on the standards:

1. *Curriculum should be ambitious and accessible.* Curricula should provide the content standards by grade levels, subjects, or courses distributed by reporting periods and by units of study. At the unit level, the standards need to be unpacked to daily learning objectives so that teachers can plan daily instruction and assessment. This provides the foundation for productive instructional planning and intentional goal-based feedback for students in the classroom every day.

2. *Instruction should be research-based and student-centered.* Teachers should plan lessons so students (1) use strategies shown to have a high probability for improving content retention and skills, (2) increase their capacity to learn independently, and (3) learn to seek productive feedback. The instruction should directly tie back to the standards and unpacked objectives; each teacher has the autonomy to design lessons, select resources, and vary delivery methods.

3. *Assessment should maximize feedback and require critical and creative thinking.* Teachers should use formative assessment to provide timely feedback, redesign assessments to require critical and creative thinking skills, and judge performance on summative assessments by standards. All assessment should directly tie back to the curriculum standards, providing the scaffolds and modifications for students to self-assess and show their best work.

4. *Feedback should track and report student progress by standards.* Teachers should use the standards-based student data gathered through formative assessment to personalize feedback, motivate improvement, and differentiate instruction for students. Equally important, it should provide accurate evidence of student learning that can be communicated to specialists, parents, and caregivers.

Many teachers will say that they already implement the Big Four. Yes, they have a curriculum, create lesson plans, use assessment techniques, and give grades. But if we ask the same teachers if all of the students perform to expectations or to the standards, most will say that they do not. A significant shift from the curriculum-instruction-assessment model to the Big Four is that teachers gauge student performance on the curriculum standards and objectives as an interactive part of instruction and assessment on a daily basis (see Figure 1.2).

FIGURE 1.2
From Traditional Framework to the Big Four

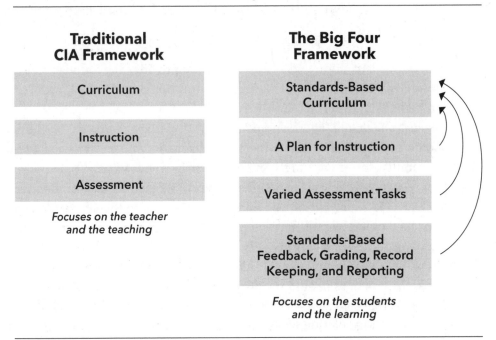

Not a New Idea

Nanos gigantum humeris insidentes, or "each generation stands on the shoulders of those who have gone before them," is an important lesson. Gary, the history teacher, asked why our generation of teachers has to use standards-based curricula or give assessments when teaching should be more of an art. The implication is that we are the first or only ones to have to do it. But, many great teachers came before us, and to deeply understand the framework we call the

Big Four, we revisit a few of the foundational elements that led to where we are today. Although there is a vast history of teaching, we chose a few of the milestones that directly tie teaching to initiatives to improve learning for all students. Remember, also, that Gary is a history teacher, so he needed to piece together the chronology; as a reader, you can skip this part if you want to get right to work on curriculum writing in Chapter 2, lesson planning in Chapter 3, assessment development in Chapter 4, or feedback approaches in Chapter 5.

In the early years of European settlement in Massachusetts, the purpose of education was to teach children to read and interpret the Bible. The Old Deluder Satan Act of 1647, and similar acts in other states, required all towns of 50 or more children to provide a community school (Ornstein, Levine, & Gutek, 1993). The intention was that all children should learn to thwart the dangerous Satan for their own well-being and for the good of the township. That law established the principles for schooling in the United States today, where the community funds and shares the responsibility for learning. Schools would prepare students through secondary school so they could attend colleges. But, despite good intentions, not all children were welcome in these schools, and those who were allowed to attend were not always able to stay in school, as they had farming, family, and later, factory duties.

More than a hundred years later, the third president, Thomas Jefferson, envisioned a country in which all citizens would be educated. Jefferson, wary of monarchial government, believed that every person should go to school to learn in order to be able to make an educated vote. To that end, schooling for all children would be the ultimate goal. As in previous generations, not all students attended school, but by the early 1900s, education laws were passed to ensure the opportunity for learning for all children. The conclusion we drew from history was that, in spite of the intention that all children would have the opportunity to go to school, many out-of-school factors prevented children from attending or completing school.

As the country edged into an Industrial Revolution at the turn of the 20th century, the need for technical education to prepare workers for specialized occupations challenged the "general knowledge" approach of schooling. This point in history pivoted the purpose for schooling to a new question: Do we design curricula that are primarily vocational in nature or primarily academic? A Committee of Ten, and later, the Commission on the Reorganization of Secondary Education, addressed the question of education's purpose in the United States. There was a general consensus that education's purpose was twofold: to support classical academics and provide readiness for the workplace. With that in mind, more children would be likely to attend school. The notion of academic and vocational programs would contribute to increased attendance and graduation rates.

World War II ended, and with the spirit of prosperity, Ralph Tyler produced an important brief that would become the pillar of school improvement for the remainder of the century. *Basic Principles of Curriculum and Instruction* (Tyler, 1949) challenged the educational community with four questions that each school should ask:

1. What educational purposes should the school seek to attain?
2. What educational experiences can the school provide to attain these purposes?
3. How can these educational experiences be effectively organized?
4. How can we determine if these purposes are being attained?

One can see the foundation of the Big Four in Tyler's questions, but keep in mind that in Tyler's time, the goal was to improve the school because it was assumed that as schools improved, so would student achievement. We find out later that, in fact, improving schools and structures does not necessarily improve learning for *all* students.

Curriculum Objectives for Educational Experiences

The post-World War II baby boom led to significant growth in the school-age population and also a call for new ways to design assessments based on the significant research gleaned from testing soldiers on specific criteria or standards for success. These ideas were consistent with Tyler's four questions to ensure successful schools.

The document, *Taxonomy of Educational Objectives*, was developed by 34 university assessment professors, edited by Benjamin Bloom, and in fact dedicated to Ralph Tyler. They suggested that in order to design better assessment, schools needed a classification system of teaching objectives to enable teachers to plan tasks and discuss learning progress toward those objectives. In other words, to create better assessments, they argued for curriculum standards. The authors clarified their intention:

> We are not attempting to classify the instructional methods used by the teachers, the ways in which teachers relate themselves to students or the different kinds of instructional materials they use. We are not attempting to classify the particular subject matter or content. What we are classifying is the intended behavior of students—the ways in which individuals are to act, think, or feel as a result of participating in some unit of instruction. (Bloom, 1956, p. 12)

By the 1950s, half of the school-age population completed secondary school, so while the intention was noble, one could argue that the results met the needs of half of the population of school-age children.

The seminal document recommending curriculum standards would lay a foundation for the curriculum part of the curriculum-instruction-assessment model. The message was that, to assess, one needs the learning target. The student learning standards proposed by Bloom and his colleagues only provided a general structure and not the precise knowledge or skills. (Teachers would have to wait 40 years, until the 1990s standards movement, to use an electronic database and disseminate comprehensive "particular subject matter or content.") Whatever the document's limitations, it established a belief system that schools should provide curriculum and assessment but leave the creativity and autonomy of lesson planning and delivery to the teacher. It seems that the idea was that if you assess the curriculum correctly, students will achieve the curriculum.

This idea of curriculum development that begins with planning for assessment, leaving teaching to the teachers, continued into the 1960s, with many authors offering methods for improvement. Robert Mager (1962) designed a way to produce "behavioral objectives." Anyone familiar with writing behavioral objectives remembers that every objective had to include the content, the assessment method, and the measurement criteria. The lengthy and complicated process required to manage all three of the components in one statement left teachers feeling overwhelmed by the sheer number of objectives written; most teachers decried the disconnect between the alleged proficiency and shallow depth of subject knowledge. Those burdensome objectives led some teachers to believe that curricula that identify clear assessment might be cumbersome, but one still has to be prepared to teach students to be active learners every day.

The curriculum-instruction-assessment model took shape as a way to improve schools. The assumption in the model was that if teachers had a written curriculum, they would teach to it and use well-designed assessments. This would result in all students learning. But, discouraged by the poor models for curriculum development and the complexity of the assessment methods, many teachers ignored curriculum, often in favor of following available textbooks. Teachers continued to make their own decisions about how to teach. At times, of course, that approach worked, but it inadvertently left subject-area gaps or created topic-area overlaps for students. Although the curriculum-instruction-assessment model for schools looked promising, not all teachers used the curriculum, and not all students performed well on the assessments.

Many unsuccessful students were able to leave school well before graduation, sometimes encouraged by retention policies.

Reexamining the Purpose of Education

By the 1970s, the effective schools movement promoted by teachers and administrators revisited Tyler's questions about schools attaining their purpose. No doubt prompted by the civil rights movement, Ronald Edmonds and others sought to improve learning for the urban poor and disenfranchised students. Among the tenets of the movement were strong school leadership, high expectations, orderly environments, basic skills, flexibility with budget and resources, and monitoring student progress. Reminiscent of the goals of previous generations, the effective schools movement sought to provide every child with the opportunity to attend an "effective school." The effective schools movement focused on the school as an organization, once more assuming that if the school were good, all the students would learn. Despite admirable efforts and great steps forward, that did not always happen. The next decade ushered in another initiative.

The 1980s introduced a new sense of urgency that forced educators to revisit Tyler's questions about schools. *A Nation at Risk*, published in 1983 by the U.S. Department of Education, appeared to hold schools responsible for the nation's predicted slide from leading the world's economy, noting that "while we can take justifiable pride in what our schools and colleges have historically accomplished and contributed to the United States and the well-being of its people, the educational foundations of our society are presently being eroded by a rising tide of mediocrity that threatens our very future as a nation and a people" (p. 1). A second report, *What Work Requires of Schools, SCANS—Report on Workplace Skills* (U.S. Department of Labor, 1991), issued a warning to parents: "Parents must insist that their sons and daughters master this [workplace] know-how and that their local schools teach it. Unless you do, your children are unlikely to earn a decent living" (p. 5).

These two reports sent teachers across the nation back to curriculum committees trying feverishly to couple the former's "new basics" with the latter's "workplace know-how." The result was a briefly used yet highly controversial type of curriculum design: outcome-based education. An *outcome* was a K–12 graduation standard that would be tested by an end-of-schooling assessment. It included subject content but was not limited to schoolwork tasks, meaning it also described appropriate preparation for the workplace. One outstanding voice during this time was Grant Wiggins, who called for changes to assessments to make them more authentic; he provided examples and generated conversations around the idea that assessment should be better than forced choice and show the breadth of students' performance abilities.

Unfortunately, outcome-based education, so ambitious but so ambiguous, riled many political and religious groups because the movement conflated academic and character education curricula with arguments about providing tax money to nonpublic schools. Although the movement failed, it prompted teachers to ask questions about how to design curricula and assessment to prepare students for both college and career.

That led to the rise of content-specific standards and grade-level benchmarks in the 1990s. Driven by the need to create a well-articulated but specific set of targets across content areas, educational organizations in the United States and many other countries published more than 150 standards documents, mobilizing to strengthen academic achievement in math, science, social studies, language arts, the fine and practical arts, and technology. Using and testing those standards became the focus of a standards movement and the assessments that would pave the way for the No Child Left Behind era.

At the risk of sounding repetitive, we note that the focus was on the school providing the curriculum standards and standardized assessments, giving teachers autonomy to plan and deliver instruction, but not all teachers knew to explicitly teach and assess to the standards, and not all children who were assessed in school performed well.

The New Century

The message of the 1990s standards movement that would lead educators into the 21st century was direct: they needed clear learning expectations, called *standards* and *grade-level benchmarks,* to describe precisely what students should know and be able to do. They were articulated across the grade levels, should be measurable through both classroom tasks and external measures, and would form the basis for reporting student progress. This was the beginning of the movement toward standards-based curriculum and report cards.

So, it seems that generations have been working on improving schools for all children for a long time: from Thomas Jefferson's Bill for the More General Diffusion of Knowledge, introduced in 1779; to Lyndon Johnson's Elementary and Secondary Education Act of 1965; to George W. Bush's No Child Left Behind signed in 2002; to the Race to the Top initiative and Every Student Succeeds Act of the 21st century in Barack Obama's administration that spotlighted schools willing to do what it would take for every child to succeed with college and careers.

Students Are Different Today

We remember being surprised when we read the statistics laid out in John Goodlad's *A Place Called School* (1984): "In 1950, only half of the white and a quarter of the black school-age population graduated from high school" (p. 12). These numbers seemed paltry for a nation that started with a vision for a fully educated population and had been ostensibly working toward that vision for close to 200 years.

One goal of education improvement is to identify which students or groups of students do not attend or complete school and figure out how to change that pattern. Historical records can be enlightening, but as we learn from Tom Snyder's *120 Years of American Education: A Statistical Portrait* (1993), attempts to examine these statistics and use them as the basis for generalizations and improvement ideas are complicated by overlapping data and shifting definitions of what it means to "complete" education. What we can say with certainty is that although public school enrollment and attendance rose significantly throughout the 20th century, rates of actual completion or graduation increased far less dramatically. In addition, those students who were enrolled, actually attended, and went on to graduate were a fairly homogeneous lot. Generally speaking, the high school graduates excluded large numbers of children living in poverty, children who worked on family farms or in family businesses, children who had physical or cognitive disabilities, children who were recent immigrants in homes with languages other than English, and those who opted out of school on their own rather than submit to the academic schedule. Additionally, those students who stayed in school until graduation were those who did well in school; those who didn't do well could be retained many years in a row and often left school without too many questions asked.

Today's classrooms are a different place. With the passage of the Individuals with Disabilities Education Act (IDEA) in 1975 and No Child Left Behind (NCLB) in 2002, teachers celebrate diversity and open the doors of public schools to all children, encouraging attendance with various forms of highly resourced supports, including creative use of technology. Appropriately, the focus of our curriculum has expanded to suit this more varied student population, and our school improvement efforts are driven by a commitment to help all the students in our classrooms learn and make progress. Nonetheless, teachers like Gary Nunnally tell us that at least four or five students, or 20–30 percent, in every class may attend, but aside from students with additional support, they do not have successful learning habits. In addition, graduation rates have hovered around that same 70–80 percent for decades. Even when the graduation rates increase, student performances on external measures indicate that many students are not proficient in literacy, mathematics, and other tested areas.

The message seems clear: something has to change in the curriculum-instruction-assessment model to work for all students.

Are Teachers Different Today?

Recently, in a professional development seminar, we asked a new teacher how she had learned to teach. Her immediate answer: "I learned from my teachers."

Teasingly, we responded, "Certainly you mean you learned from your college professors?"

"No," she replied confidently, "I mean from watching my school teachers."

If you agree with this teacher, and with a premise put forth by Jim Stigler, coauthor (with James Hiebert) of *The Teaching Gap* (1999) and (with Harold Stevenson) *The Learning Gap* (1992), you believe that we learned the habit of teaching by watching our own elementary and secondary teachers. When we were sitting in classrooms as students, day after day, year after year, we were building and solidifying habits that defined teaching for us. These habits made it difficult for us to significantly change behaviors once we started teaching. So, if we learned to teach from our teachers, and they learned to teach from their teachers, and so on, one could argue that many of us today have teaching habits that stretch back to the 1970s, when graduation rates hovered at 70 percent. Add to that, anyone who learned to teach from those teachers carried the same habits into the 1980s and, yes, to today's teachers.

It might be stated that our teaching and assessment strategies were inherited from teachers who were responsible for instructing only three-quarters of today's students, and they were less diverse than classrooms today. We call that *pedagogical automaticity* and will discuss it more in Chapter 3. We show how slight changes to habits of planning and delivering instruction can improve learning for all students.

To help students succeed today, we need to incorporate a few different learning tools. However, we should not forget that the teaching tools used in previous generations *did work for many students.* As we developed the Big Four, we kept the components of the older models that worked and only made changes based on current research about learning. The Big Four shifts the focus from improving the school system to improving individual student learning. Secondly, it assumes that the curriculum has to be well enough defined that teachers find it useful for planning their instruction and classroom assessment. Finally, the Big Four recommends standards-based scoring to provide motivation and record keeping as a way to ensure better feedback to students so they are more likely to perform to standards.

Looking Ahead

The lessons in this book are about slightly changing teaching habits where the learning happens day by day.

Chapter 1 is a detailed introduction to the Big Four. It acknowledges that past practices in improving student learning have been based on hope rather than certainty: "I *hope* this lesson works." "I *hope* the students will do the homework." "I *hope* the class will do well on the test." The Big Four is not entirely a new idea but instead updates previous frameworks. The Big Four approach offers (1) clear, well-paced curriculum standards that describe what students will learn, (2) research-based daily lesson planning for delivery within units of study, (3) redesigned assessments for critical and creative thinking skills as well as formative assessment that provides timely feedback to students, and (4) tracking individual progress to the standards to provide more accurate feedback, differentiation, and reporting.

Chapter 2 begins the focused examination of the first of the Big Four tenets. The curriculum development process described in the chapter can help any teacher or curriculum specialist create documents or manage revisions to guides that inform daily planning. Gone are the days of creating the old boxy forms that generate pages of empty columns. The new format is efficient, streamlined, and consistent with viewing online or print documents.

Chapter 3 zooms in on how to plan and deliver instruction to maximize student engagement and learning. It describes an approach to lesson planning and delivery that was adapted from Hunter's *Mastery Teaching* (1982) and identified as a teaching schema for master learners. The first important change in the new approach (referred to by the acronym GANAG) is the idea of planning lessons so that students use nine high-yield strategies from *Classroom Instruction That Works* (Marzano, Pickering, & Pollock, 2001). The chapter describes that when teachers plan using a schema based on how to teach, their focus inadvertently centers on what they accomplish as teachers; but, using the new lesson planning schema based on how learners learn, the teacher focuses on student learning. Today with the knowledge of how humans learn based on newer studies and improved neuroscience, we can apply that knowledge to lesson planning and delivery.

The second critical aspect to the lesson schema is how it guides teachers to decide whether they will teach procedural knowledge, which requires practice, or declarative knowledge, which requires teaching students to use critical and creative thinking skills. Most curriculum involves declarative knowledge, so teachers should plan lessons that guide students to use thinking skills to deepen learning, increase questioning, and provide for more robust project-based learning.

Chapters 4 and 5 discuss two different aspects of assessment described by the Big Four. In the traditional curriculum-instruction-assessment frame-work, all assessment is bundled. We address different types of assessment tasks in Chapter 4 and the timing of feedback, standards-based record keep-ing, and reporting in Chapter 5.

In addition to exploring a primary theme, each chapter in this book gives teachers and specialists an opportunity to voice how they use the Big Four approach in their own teaching. They share their experiences and those of their colleagues, relating anecdotes of enthusiasm, challenge, and change. Each notes the reward of patiently transforming teaching in order to improve student learning.

Summary

The Big Four, as we will learn in the following chapters, modifies practices evolved from the work of researchers and practitioners from J. F. Herbart in the 1800s, to Ralph Tyler and Benjamin Bloom in the next mid-century, to Grant Wiggins and Madeline C. Hunter in the late 20th century. Each contrib-uted enormously to the field, and each new publication seemed to provide the one perfect solution for school improvement; however, most of the previous recommendations were intended to fix the system, the leadership, and school structures, hoping that would ensure that all students learn well.

Curriculum-instruction-assessment guided teaching toward the goal to becoming master teachers. Today teachers can apply research to update that model to the Big Four, which focuses on students becoming master learners. To improve learning, and not just hope new structures and systems will work, one can focus directly on what happens every day in the classroom. In the 21st century we have new answers to the question about how humans learn, so we should be able to approach classrooms by shifting the focus from what makes a good teacher to what makes good learning happen for every student every day.

Teacher Voice
Gary Nunnally, *Middle and High School Social Studies Teacher in Nebraska*

I had to be dragged kicking and screaming to "one more PD" session a number of years ago. I planned to grade papers, but not because I didn't care or was intentionally trying to be the resistant teacher. I truly believed that grading papers was key to improving my students' learning. In my mind, grading papers was much more vital to my students' learning than attending another meeting and adding one more thing to my to-do list, on top of all the other responsibilities I already had as a classroom teacher. After nearly a decade of teaching middle and high school students, professional development sessions had become one of the least important parts of my job; I had developed the attitude of "this too shall pass."

What made this session different from all the others I had previously attended was the effect the training would have on my career that would benefit the hundreds of students I have taught since. It began with the presenter, Jane Pollock, sharing a seemingly harmless but illuminating question: "I ask myself, would my classroom be good enough for my sons?" I was completely taken aback.

At the time I had two children, Joshua and Elizabeth, so I quickly adapted the question to the "Josh and Ellie test." Would my lesson today be good enough if Josh and Ellie were in my class? I had to acknowledge that although I worked hard and wanted to be as effective a teacher as possible, I was falling short. I looked at the papers I was grading and realized that many of the students were not doing well. What if Josh or Ellie were not doing well and all they got back was red-marked papers telling them what they had done wrong?

As difficult as it is to admit, in that moment I came to the realization that my own classroom was not passing the Josh and Ellie test.

So, I raised my hand in that PD session, surprising myself and all of my friends in the back row, and asked, "Are you going to tell us how to do it?"

My Big Four Transformation

I was and continue to be a work in progress. It reminds me of Coach John Wooden's words: "It's what you learn after you know it all that really counts," and, "Once you are finished learning, you are finished." This description about my four-year transformation does not indicate a state of "arrival." However, it's helpful to examine the first four years (other teachers don't take four years for this process—I was a slow learner!) of my transformation in my classroom, where it is easy to trace the specific changes to my pedagogical automaticity.

Year 1: Listening and Learning. I'm embarrassed now to say that, before my transformation, every year I was already tired by October. I was tired of the same conversations producing the same results—tired of the same four or five kids failing, the same kids being disengaged from learning, and the same kids causing the same classroom management problems. None of these problems was fully remedied in my first year of using the Big Four approach, but the process of transforming my classroom had begun. I was dutifully attending the training sessions about instructional planning, taking notes, and asking a lot of questions. In addition, I was beginning to rewrite, not just edit, my lesson plans using a new lesson schema that focused on teaching students to be master learners (and helping students achieve specific goals), but also working at changing my practices in order to be a master teacher.

Toward the end of year 1, the lesson planning process convinced me to stop giving points for homework because, in truth, we were getting a lot more work done in class by incorporating a research-based routine. In the past, the loss of so many homework points for so many students caused grades to fall. Then, I would give extra assignments to get their grades up and also have to explain why some students could pass tests but had failing grades. This first step was a difficult one for me. I did not really understand the whole process, and I gave up the homework points practice reluctantly. To be certain, I was not yet ready to stop giving points for quizzes and projects! At this juncture, I naively thought the problem in my classroom was the points for homework. And I was fixing that. I still gave some homework and we still marked it, but it was considered formative, whatever that meant.

Year 2: From Points to Performance. During the second year, I began planning with another 7th grade history teacher. Yes, I finally cracked open the proverbial "closed door." (You know the one: "This is my classroom, this is how I've always taught, and this is how I'm going to continue teaching with my door closed.") Once a week, this colleague and I got together during our planning time and mapped out where we were headed with our students that week. While we coplanned all year together, I also rewrote my assessments so that I was testing and grading to the district-provided standards to which we were both teaching based on the new lesson schema. My coplanner thought I was crazy to use only tests (not homework, participation, and behavior) to determine students' grades, but because he saw the benefit of planning together, we at least continued to meet.

That year, I assigned my first project without any "points," just grading to the standards and benchmarks. Before I gave my students the assignment, I called my friend Gerry Larson at district staff development for moral support. I said, "Let me make sure that I've got this straight. I am going to give more than 140 middle school students a project that will take about one week to complete, and I am not going to make it worth any points. What will motivate them if they cannot earn points?" Gerry calmly reminded me that I was scoring to the benchmarks, not gathering (and taking away) points. As I hung up the phone, I felt a combination of emotions—fear, as well as a tinge of "Hey, something exciting is happening here." As I look back on it, it was a very freeing feeling. I was beginning to emerge from my self-imposed reliance on points—beginning to let the benchmarks guide not just my teaching but also students' learning.

As I delivered the project instructions to my students, I broke out in a sweat. I had visions of my principal walking through the door and seeing my students completely off-task, standing on desks, singing, dancing, and totally out of control. I just knew I was going to get fired. And then, the epiphany: I had not been using the assessment process to improve student achievement; I had been using points to *control student behavior*.

And, wouldn't you know it, my students appeared motivated to complete the assignment the same way they would have under the old points system. That is, some students produced exemplary projects, many completed the assignment satisfactorily, and a number of students performed unacceptably. Although I'd taken a critical step toward implementing the GANAG schema, I felt I was still teaching in much the same way I had before, except without the security blanket of "points," I would need to make more changes before the level of my students' learning truly transformed.

I created a rubric to assess students and guide their work to help them know what an incomplete, emerging, proficient, and exemplary project would look like. There would be no points assigned as "grade boosters" (e.g., points for presentation, timeliness, and so on). To my surprise, more students stayed on pace with their projects, including the ones who would have disengaged earlier. Students actually started seeking my feedback about their understandings of content because they were not distracted by collecting points along the way to the finished product. And, they were motivated to learn, not collect points.

This was the first time in eleven years that every student in class finished the project on time.

A Recovering Gradeaholic

I write today as a recovering *gradeaholic*. Ralph Waldo Emerson said, "Rings and other jewels are not gifts, but apologies. The only gift is a portion of thyself." Giving "a portion of thyself" can mean many things for a teacher. One thing it definitely means is *time*.

I did not have more time than any other teacher. But as I employed the Big Four, I no longer spent the majority of my time grading every assignment, assigning numbers or points for completion, and taking off points for things like tardiness (and trying to figure out what percentage of points should be taken off if the assignment is one or two days late, one week late, etc.). Instead, I spent that time with my students, focusing on their learning and enjoying teaching as a planning, delivery, and assessment/feedback process. I also learned how to use scoring to the standards frequently as a reteaching tool. Consistently and systematically employing the Big Four to my teaching allowed me to group my students during class, my strugglers and my high achievers, and provide substantial reteaching and enrichment based on their performance on the standards. Through the use of student self-assessment on the goal of the lesson, my students knew up front what it is they needed to know or do. Through the use of GANAG, the new schema, and the high-yield strategies, I was helping my students to become master learners. And, I used assessment and feedback strategies to motivate rather than discourage learning in my classroom. Yes!

I took the elimination of points a step further and began giving students quizzes that were not worth any points. Of course, my students would invariably ask, "Mr. Nunnally, how much is number two worth? How many points should I take off for missing number three?" I would calmly reply that I did not want them to take any points off; I wanted them to understand what they had missed so they could make the necessary improvements. I would urge them to fill in the answer correctly, making sure they knew why they had missed it. I reminded students that the most successful people know what they know and what they do not know and work hard to learn what they do not know. This new way of grading was a continuous learning process for my kids. It took some students longer to get it than others. Sometimes, in exasperation, I would tell students, "Fine, today's quiz is worth 5,000 points," or, "Take 100 points off if you miss number four!" Usually this helped to clarify the goal; it was about learning, not about accumulating more points for a final grade.

Just because I was not giving points for daily work, projects, and quizzes doesn't mean that my students were not receiving feedback, nor does it mean that there were no points assigned for test performance. Since I was a basketball coach, I would tell my students, "Friday night, the lights will be on, the town and the cheerleaders will be there, and we'll be keeping score. In the meantime, continue to work hard at your preparation so you'll be ready for your performance on the test." Then, when the students got ready to take their exam, I no longer said, "Good luck." Instead, I said, "I hope that you perform as well as you have prepared." Invariably students would say, "So you want me to fail?" I would smile and calmly reply, "No, I want you to understand the importance of effort and preparation, and then I want your grade to simply be a reflection of your learning. I want what you learn in my class to help you be successful in life, not just social studies." Student grades were improving as the semester went on, and I found that "It's all about feedback; improvement is all about frequent feedback to 'just-right' standards and then instructional time to make improvements."

Year 3: The Dip. During the third year of transformation, I accepted a new job in a different district, purely for family reasons. I was excited about the new job and about the district. But before too long, my excitement was drained by the teaching approach favored by my new school.

Remember the Wendy's commercial featuring an elderly lady yelling, "Where's the beef?" As I began preparing my lesson plans, I wanted to yell, "Where are the standards?" For two years, I had worked hard to reassess my teaching and create lesson plans that began with clearly stated standards and objectives. Now I had moved to a new district that expected me to teach thematically without a clear standards-based curriculum.

This expectation posed a new challenge. I worked hard to implement the expectations of my district while at the same time putting together a curriculum document on my own. I understand the frustration of the teacher who doesn't have a clear set of curriculum standards and objectives. I also realized the enormous value in having curriculum documents that didn't just sit on the shelf, and when I found myself in a situation without a clear set of targets, I went to work creating them. My curriculum documents became a living document, one that I would take notes on, revise, and continue to align with our state standards. Then, I could use my curriculum documents on a daily basis as I created my daily lessons, my varied assessments, and my record keeping.

I also worked to ensure that my formative assessments were aligned with the standards, and my feedback helped students make improvements on the standards.

A new addition to my pedagogy emerged: I asked to team with our media specialist. After a typical exam, I would spend the next day with the students who were not proficient in achieving the learning objectives. Our media specialist would provide enrichment activities and lessons for the students who had already performed at a proficient level on their learning objectives. For instance, at the time, I taught 7th grade world history. Our first unit was a geography unit. The students who performed at a proficient level got to make a "trading card" of a country, similar to baseball or football trading cards, complete with fascinating facts about that country. I laminated the cards for them. I knew I was onto something when the students who had to retest (and, thus, had missed out on the enrichment activity) asked if they could make a card on their own and have me laminate it for them. I thought to myself, "This is interesting; my students are asking me if they can do more school work and it isn't even worth any points." I would also note that there have been times that the media specialist was not able to team with me and I simply provided enrichment and reteaching/retesting myself in my classroom. Now, this was a process that was passing the Josh and Ellie test!

Year 4: The Lights Are On and the Town and the Cheerleaders Are Cheering. The fourth year of my transformation brought an amazing, and utterly unexpected, revelation: my principal came into the classroom to observe me, and I realized I was teaching the lesson the same way I would on any other day! For years I had fretted over my lesson when I knew my principal would be observing me. How could I make the lesson *really* exciting? How could I make sure my students were *really* engaged in their learning that day? Maybe they would have mercy on me, notice the principal was there, and at least *act* like they were interested and learning. Instead, during this fourth year, I made lesson plans using the new schema, as I do every other day of the year, and taught the lesson without worrying about the presence of my principal; I had achieved a new pedagogical automaticity. There was nothing out of the ordinary about the lesson that day—just rich conversations with my students as we discussed and engaged in the learning process together. What a feeling!

The Resistance

When I changed districts during that third year of my transformation, part of my new job was to coach the school's basketball team, with the clear expectation on my part (and the administration's) that I was coming to build the program into championship form. At the beginning of our first year together, the team and I established our theme for the basketball program: "New Season...New Dreams." During that first year, people would frequently tell me, "You can't do this; you can't do that; we've never done it that way before." I would then explain that one definition of insanity is to do things the way they've always been done and expect different results. In other words, if they expected different results from the basketball team, as I did, then we really did need to make this a new season with new dreams and work hard to achieve them. The resistance to the transformation in my classroom had been no less intense.

I remember realizing that when I truly started adhering to the Big Four principles, my classroom experience became much more intense. It reminded me of the intensity of a well-planned and executed basketball practice. As the teacher, I really was ultimately responsible for how my students did. No longer would grades be "padded" by daily work and extra credit. My students' grades would simply reflect their learning. Now that I was assessing to the standards, I could pinpoint where students were struggling and determine if I needed to make changes to my curriculum documents, my instructional planning or delivery, or perhaps my formative assessments. If my students were failing, they were not learning; and if they were not learning, it was my job to help them improve their learning! No longer could I think or say, "Well, if the student would just turn in his or her homework...."

Meet the Parents

Back in year 2, members of my 7th grade team asked me to come to a meeting to compile a list of our students who were failing. We would mail a letter home to parents advising them that their child was failing. Then they would receive a mid-quarter report that invariably showed their child was still failing. We followed up in both cases to make sure the parents had received the notices, ensuring that they and the students were advised before receiving the final quarter grade.

Now, what educator or parent can deny the importance of maintaining open communication with parents? It is certainly important that parents are properly apprised of their child's standing in class. My point is not to knock my team members' efforts at communication. But these were conversations about points, and lack of points, rather than conversations about student learning.

When I informed my team members that, in fact, I did not have any failing students (for the first time in 10 years of teaching middle and high school students), I was met with a combination of disbelief and scorn. ("Nunnally must really be lowering his standards!") My alienation was only compounded when the team replied, "That's OK, just come and write letters to the parents of the kids who have zeroes for not turning in assignments," and I had to tell them that I didn't have any students with zeroes. (These days, my students process all of their assignments in an individual notebook, which is a work in progress. They can always go back and add to their notes and improve their learning.) When I look back on these experiences, I realize that although they were motivated by good intentions, all of the meetings and notifications were just smoke and mirrors—a replacement for real learning and progress.

Given my experiences, I can appreciate the importance of implementing change in a team environment with administrative support. At the time, I was alone among my colleagues, trying to make massive changes to my pedagogy alone. How empowering it is to be at a school where my principal is an instructional leader, encouraging positive changes that are based on sound research-based principles.

Many people have asked me about the response my students' parents have had to my Big Four transformation. In the past, I was always nervous about parent–teacher conferences. How would the parents respond to their child failing? What would they think of the zeroes their child had received and the resultant effect on her overall grade? Well, by the end of the second year of the transformation, I was looking forward to parent–teacher conferences. Just as I did in the classroom, I made the focus of the conference the child's learning (or lack thereof) rather than a discussion of the many points needed to make a grade. With their grades now determined by learning tied to specific standards, the entire process of teaching and learning held so much more integrity for me, for the student, and for the parents, which opened up a whole new realm of communication in parent–teacher conferences.

Low-Performing Students

Let me write for a moment about the low-performing student who has been caught in a cycle of failure. Not only have that child's parents heard the same report from every teacher, but they have probably heard the same report year after year after year: "Lee won't turn in assignments and has numerous zeroes for late papers, and this has resulted in a lowering of his grade." Imagine the moment when these parents sit across from me: I show them a report that focuses on their child's demonstration of learning and explain that their child has earned a *C* or a *B*—or sometimes even an *A*.

The response from parents has certainly differed. Some have raised their lowered eyes and asked incredulously, "Are you *sure* this is Lee's grade?" Some have almost broken down in tears. Others have responded that their child "just likes your class." To which I invariably reply, "That cannot be. Remember, I teach history!" For some parents, after seeing how my class is set up, the response is, "Wow, my child would have to try not to pass your course. You tell them up front what they need to know and be able to do, teach them the importance of effort and tracking their progress on specific learning goals, provide feedback every day to them on their learning goals, formally provide feedback through the use of formative assessments, and provide an opportunity for retesting when they fall short on a specific standard!" (Yes!)

Teaming with the Special Education Department

Another benefit of utilizing the Big Four was the efficiency created working with our special education department. These are teachers who are heroically trying to guide their students through the myriad of expectations and school work in multiple classes. For some, I think it is about helping their students "do school better." By varying assessments, we were truly able to individualize their learning and help them learn at a progressing level. My final year in the classroom I had five students with special needs in one class period. Toward the end of the year, our special education director stopped by and asked to see my fifth period roster. She was astonished when she found out 25 percent of my class had special needs and I didn't have another teacher in my classroom, and I wasn't experiencing the same classroom management issues with these students that some teachers found. For the entire semester I had patiently worked with these five students to help them understand that it wasn't about "doing school right" in my classroom. It truly was about their learning and that ultimately their grade was based on how well they learned. It was very satisfying that, by the end of the year, four of these five students began coming to me for extra help, asking questions, seeking my feedback on their notebooks, and correcting mistakes in their notebooks as they prepared for their formative and summative assessments. And, finally, they realized that they could not raise their grade by turning in more assignments or doing extra credit work; in order to improve their grade, they had to improve their learning. I had hoped the fifth would eventually come along, but excessive absences and major personal issues prevented him from receiving the instruction and teaching he needed to be able to pass; he was able to get support in other ways. I have to admit that prior to my implementation of the Big Four, many more students would have, and did, fail my courses.

High-Performing Students

Does anyone else have high school students who miss multiple days of school, especially in the springtime with the multitude of sports and activities? For me, many of these students were high-performing students involved in a variety of activities. In the past, these students would have frustratingly asked what they had to do to get caught up, or the classic "I am going to be gone the next two days—are we doing anything?" Now that I had successfully implemented the Big Four, these students would access the lesson and their history, economics, or government textbook online and begin processing their learning in their notebooks; in some cases, they could access video from a lesson so they could follow along, guided by the class and my direct instruction. They would write their learning goal at the top of their page and then begin accessing their prior knowledge. After reading and applying new information by practicing or applying a thinking skill, the students would summarize and score their learning. When they returned to school, I didn't have to hunt them down to make sure they did their schoolwork. Instead, these students would seek me out to provide some feedback, either verbally or through in-class scoring with the focus on their learning of the standards.

I am struck by the reminder that every student who walked through my door is someone's Josh or Ellie. If, as educators, we know that there are certain methods proven to improve student achievement, and we use them to implement these changes in our own classrooms, we are able to make the difference in our students' lives that we all seek to do. Every child who passes through our doors deserves our very best efforts; they are all equally deserving of lessons, assessments, and feedback that pass the Josh and Ellie test.

Today

When I ask teachers, "What is one strategy you use to improve students learning?" I get a variety of reasonable responses such as improved note taking, better home life, technology, and so forth. The problem is that I can't necessarily affect these areas. I encourage them to focus on those things they can control as they work to improve the learning of all of their students. My response is that if I could do one thing, I would be a one-on-one tutor for all of my students. Short of that, I would work to employ the Big Four to share clear learning objectives based on standards, students' consistent and systematic use of high-yield strategies, varied formative and summative assessment, and feedback to the standards. Every day, every child, I am helping each student become a master learner.

2

Curriculum Design from Standards to Units to Daily Lessons

Belinda Parini was excited to be named the lead teacher for curriculum in the building where she had worked for the previous 10 years. Her principal asked her to convene the subject-area leaders in an effort to set the direction for the year to improve student learning and, more specifically, test scores. To this first meeting, teacher leaders were asked to bring curriculum documents, including assessments, used in their departments.

Looking back, Belinda remembered the incredibly uncomfortable feeling that infiltrated the room when a few subject-area leaders described how they had tried to find curriculum documents on a shared drive but were not successful. One chairperson produced not one but *four* versions of their subject curriculum documents. The first version was created when the state officially adopted a set of standards, with a format of four columns across that showed standards, activities, assessments, and resources. The second version for the same subject was a hybrid that included the standards in units; the teachers said they liked that better, but upon viewing the document, they noticed that not all of the standards were chosen and most of the units were missing assessments. One teacher, they said, used a version she found in the shared drive, but others clarified that was the old document and it no longer aligned to the state assessments. The fourth document, identified by a teacher as *the one,* was the most recent state version, but it was still in draft form and would not be adopted until the following school year and the testing component not for two years, so no one in the department was ready to consider this version an option.

Belinda offered that in her subject area—physical education and health— teachers had been told they could use either the state or national standards, so some of the course curricula had both, while others did not document any standards at all. She also added that when subject-area leaders did share their examples, the differences among the formats were apparent, especially in content breadth and depth, which led to inconsistent use across the school.

Does this sound familiar? It is a scene that we have seen play out at countless schools during curriculum work time, and it has led many teachers to protest that they want to be curriculum *users,* not curriculum *writers.* Individual teachers often hunt through document files, print and digital, to cobble together a curriculum that they often keep on their own computers but do not necessarily update on a shared drive. At the session described, one of Belinda's colleagues declared that although it would be nice if they had the documents, there were so many other schoolwide initiatives to address that no one really had time to "do the curriculum" or update any of the online units. Few teachers, they said, used the curriculum to guide their teaching.

While many teachers say they appreciate useful curriculum documents providing grade-level or course expectations, they also admit that they find them time-consuming to produce. Many of the state or provincial documents online require lots of clicks to access different pages for files, or they appear in such complex formats that it takes a lot of time to extract their grade-level or course information. We hear teachers reminisce about the time when they would get together for a couple of days every other summer to write the curriculum. They would put the documents in a three-ring binder on a shelf that would, unfortunately, gather dust. Belinda was pretty sure that their online documents were gathering cyber dust.

Now what was she supposed to do? To improve student learning and subsequently test scores, teachers want to have a firm grasp on what students know and are able to do in comparison to the learning expectations (curriculum). But there seemed to be no commonly agreed-upon, easily accessible, and readable sets of learning expectations or standards. Without them, the lesson planning and delivery (instruction), the demonstrations of learning (assessment), and the transfer of information through coaching (feedback) would likely be arbitrary and maintain the status quo. Belinda sought to remove this barrier between curriculum and teachers so the most important end users—the students—could benefit from direct alignment of instruction, assessment, and feedback to the curriculum.

Making Curriculum Useful

Remember Benjamin Bloom and the university examiners from the 1950s who proposed that the way to improve student learning was to give educators a classification system of educational goals to promote the exchange of the best ideas and materials? They wrote that the well-informed classroom teacher would use the taxonomy as a guidepost for professional conversations. The conversations would lead to better teaching, better assessment, and better learning for all students. They argued for curricula to guide teaching to improve student learning. Sounds familiar. In the 1950s, using the technology available to them, they produced a brief but powerful sample of educational objectives, intended as a model so teachers and schools could produce their own. The curriculum initiatives since then have included behavioral objectives, outcomes, and finally the standards movement in the United States.

In each case, teachers were expected to use the curriculum statements to devise curriculum documents that would guide their lesson planning. It doesn't feel like much has changed since the 1980s when Fenwick W. English called out the format of curriculum documents as one of at least five reasons the "guides are a wasteful expenditure of educational resources" (English, 1986). In addition to being in a user-unfriendly format (what he calls the "formidable bulk"), English went on to question the caliber of curriculum guides due to

- The lack of identified indicators of quality for the documents;
- The notion that the teachers must actually write the curriculum when, in practice, many teachers find themselves following a textbook;
- The belief that curriculum writing is a "never-ending process" absent of deadlines and accountability measures; and
- The disconnect between educational strategic planning at the local, regional, and state levels and the operational realities at the school and classroom levels.

English's plea for the curriculum development process to be "scaled down… become shorter and more compact… and [to] become smaller and more usable" unfortunately still resonates today (English, 1986).

Teachers often remark that writing curriculum is daunting, and with so many lessons to plan, curriculum documents never seem to get *done*. When we ask why, they describe a cumbersome overload of information required to peruse and templates with so many fields that need to be filled in. Making the documents has dampened, if not extinguished, enthusiasm among teachers for both using and revising them on a regular basis. Inevitably, a disconnect between producing the curriculum and using it has naturally occurred, as current documents—no matter their version as seen in Belinda's experience—are often viewed explicitly or implicitly as unusable by many teachers. Curriculum writing also tends to be exclusive, taking place in the summer when not all can attend, or with small groups of teachers during the school year when planning time and substitute teachers are scarce. Teachers can be hesitant to use, let alone revise, curriculum created by others. How might we shift this paradigm?

It's the Format

Many curriculum documents are still formatted in what we might call the "old way." Whether print or electronic, most templates include headers framed into boxes for big ideas, essential questions, and standards followed by objectives, learning activities, assessments, and resources, organized into tables with multiple columns, or dispersed into data fields across various web pages within a software program. These arrangements usually feature text so compressed by space constraints or found within different areas of the software application that it is difficult to read or follow the overall scope and sequence. Our pet peeve is the four or five pages of blank columns with only one filled in; the text in the one column is strangely hyphenated because of the format of the file. Individual teachers, grade-level teams, and subject-area departments then find themselves creating additional documents in order to turn the unfriendly formats into unit and lesson plans—many times independently and saved on their own devices.

Teachers tell us that they should be able to go online, access a file that shows the subject-area goals for the unit and week, and write or modify lessons. Curriculum writing should produce streamlined files for teachers to reference when planning their lessons (see Figure 2.1). A teacher should be able to spend less time wrestling with paragraph-length standards or extraneous details and more time planning great instruction for students.

Listening to teachers across grade levels and subjects, and keeping in mind the criteria for the Big Four, we discovered that using today's technology to change the typical format of the curriculum documents might be the key to improving both development and usage. Here we will share *the curriculum secret*. We are joking about a secret, but as you will see below, the key to formatting is the "deleting" process. The tools needed to create this type of robust, usable curriculum are what most schools already have in place: personal computing devices (e.g., desktop computers, laptops), a productivity suite that includes word processing and spreadsheet programs (e.g., Microsoft Office, Google Docs), and a shared digital repository (e.g., Google Drive, SharePoint).

Let's get started.

FIGURE 2.1
Curriculum Files Organization

1. The overall course document
   • Standards
   • Course description
2. The year or semester at a glance
   • Unit titles
3. The pacing matrix (optional)
   • Standards distributed across terms (or units)
4. The standards distributed by reporting period
5. The unit plans
   • Unpacked standards
   • Summative and formative assessments tools
   • Resources (print and online)

---

1. The Overall Course Document

Whether it is for the pre-calculus course in 11th grade, the digital media offering in 7th grade, or the science class in 1st grade, a course or grade-level document is the general standards document. All of the other files will depend on this one to save time and error through the deleting process. Traditionally, the following components are included in the overall standards document (see Figure 2.2), but certainly you can change them to meet your school's needs:

- The name of the course or grade-level subject
- The grade level(s) when the course is either required or usually taken
- The term length of the course (e.g., quarter, trimester, semester, yearlong)
- The prerequisite course(s) or conditions that must be met to enroll in the course
- The course description
- The standards for the course
- The chosen textbook, guide, and/or online resources recommended to teachers

FIGURE 2.2

Mathematics Course Document for Grade 7 Sample

MATHEMATICS
Middle School Division-Grade 7

MA

Course Description

Critical thinking skills developed in 7th grade mathematics not only benefit students who pursue further studies and careers within the field, it supports all students by strengthening problem solving, logic, and reasoning abilities for success with life's daily tasks like calculating costs and finding the best deals when shopping. Students explore ratios and proportional relationships; add, subtract, multiply, and divide rational numbers and integers; solve inequalities; apply pre-algebra to geometry concepts; and use statistics and probability to draw inferences. Through the practice of skills and application of concepts to real-world situations, students are introduced to pre-algebra content.

Prerequisite: Mathematics - Grade 6
Standards Source: The Common Core State Standards (Mathematics)
Resource: <<title of primary resource(s), such as textbook, online resource(s), etc.>>

Standards

7.RP.1. Compute unit rates associated with ratios of fractions, including ratios of lengths, areas, and other quantities measured in like or different units. For example, if a person walks 1/2 mile in each 1/4 hour, compute the unit rate as the complex fraction 1/2 / 1/4 miles per hour, equivalently 2 miles per hour.

7.RP.2. Recognize and represent proportional relationships between quantities.

7.RP.3. Use proportional relationships to solve multistep ratio and percent problems. Examples include simple interest, tax, markups and markdowns, gratuities and commissions, fees, percent increase and decrease, percent error.

7.NS.1. Apply and extend previous understandings of addition and subtraction to add and subtract rational numbers; represent addition and subtraction on a horizontal or vertical number line diagram.

7.NS.2. Apply and extend previous understandings of multiplication and division and of fractions to multiply and divide rational numbers.

7.NS.3. Solve real-world and mathematical problems involving the four operations with rational numbers. (Computations with rational numbers extend the rules for manipulating fractions to complex fractions.)

7.EE.1. Apply properties of operations as strategies to add, subtract, factor, and expand linear expressions with rational coefficients.

7.EE.2. Understand that rewriting an expression in different forms in a problem context can shed light on the problem and how the quantities in it are related. For example, a + 0.05a = 1.05a means that "increase by 5%" is the same as "multiply by 1.05."

Adapted from Common Core State Standards, 2010b.

We begin by preparing the standards and will then add the headers, including the school logo, course description, and details, and the footers that might include page numbers, citations, and the version date. Figure 2.2 shows the first page of a finished version.

From a schoolwide perspective in particular, all of the aforementioned components have a purpose and may be determined at the teacher, school, or district level. If a teacher is working alone, he can prepare his own course documents following the exact same steps. We'd like to take a closer look at a couple of these components in which teacher participation in the document's preparation is critical: the standards and the course description.

The Standards. A standards-based curriculum intends to connect each of the grade-level or course standards to the standards in the grade levels above and below or the courses preceding and following it; a teacher's curriculum is a link in a chain from preschool to grade 12 connected by standards. Identifying standards, then, is the starting point in creating this chain. Many teachers are required by their school or state to subscribe to a particular set. Standards can also be easily found online from states, provinces, countries, or groups, such as the subject-area experts that developed the National Core Arts Standards.

It is worth noting that since the first edition of this book was published, the terminology used when referring to standards has shifted. In the past, different levels of specificity were referred to uniquely, from standard (the overarching PK–12 subject-area statement) to benchmark (the grade-level manifestation of the standard) to indicator (evidence of understanding that the benchmark had been achieved). Now when referring to a standard, teachers are, for the most part, referring to the grade-level or course-specific learning progression that has been identified or adopted for a specific grade level or course, which is relatively equivalent to the benchmark of days past. When we use the word *standard* in this book, we refer to the grade-level or course learning goal that later will be unpacked for daily use.

The grade-level or course-specific standards, such as the state standards, national standards, or the Next Generation Science Standards, are vertically aligned learning progressions. Fortunately, most sets of standards can be accessed online. Teachers working in independent schools might have more flexibility on their choices and should view various documents, even blending them.

To start, we recommend downloading the appropriate standards for the grade level or course. Note that most transfers result in tables and spacing that make the standards document feel and look disheveled. In about 45 minutes, using a simple cut and paste into a word processing document, the electronic layout can be adjusted to a very basic format. We want to highlight here that the format is imperative.

1. Align text to the left.
2. Have little to no indenting or tabs.
3. Use one font style and size.
4. Number the standards with an uncomplicated coding system.

This structure makes a standards document formatted for us to start the "deleting" process later when we create the reporting period documents and the units of study. The reason for keeping the formatting to a minimum is to be able to easily manage the document without the columns, rows, fonts, and other distracting elements; most important, it allows for the teacher to get right to work on instruction and assessment design. We believe in making it simple: copy from the online source, paste into a word processing document, format to a basic layout, add the headers/footers, and move on to prepare the other documents.

The Course Description. The course description is a short summary about the content for the course or the grade level. Typically organized by grade levels in the primary years and subject areas from the middle years onward, the standards can be examined and summarized by a teacher (or a group of teachers who all teach a common course) into a short description or statement that provides brief information about the topics or skills learned in the course. No more than a paragraph long, it should describe the course's or level's contents.

One benefit to having teachers write the course descriptions and review them on an annual basis is that it provides a purposeful opportunity for them to either be introduced to a new set of standards they have chosen or are expected to use, or review the ones currently in place. When done as a grade-level team or at the department level, a platform for collaboration is established for calibration purposes, particularly for the subsequent conversation that is to determine which standards are essential for a course and which standards may need to be adapted for a local reason, such as student needs, a school improvement focus, or a state recommendation. And, of course, if a new set of standards is adopted locally, a revision or full rewrite of the course description may be necessary, including the reference information to chosen standards. In essence, this work of summarizing provides time for teachers to gain clarity and come to agreement about course content: what is and what is not included in the offering.

Another advantage of this writing exercise, especially at the secondary level, is that course descriptions can then be compiled into a program of studies for the school system that can be shared with students at registration time, for parents to know what their child is learning at that grade level or in a course, and, with colleges and universities, as evidence of a viable, aligned curriculum.

To complete the overall document, teachers can paste the header, which includes the course description and other details such as the timeframe, essential questions or big ideas, and prerequisites, onto the first page of the file, and the footer, which includes the page numbers and possibly the bibliographic information about the standards and date of the version.

2. The Year or Semester at a Glance

This step is important because it gives many teachers the chance to maintain the integrity of their previous curriculum processes and dignifies the work they have done in the past. We ask teachers to list the unit titles they have taught in the past in the sequence they prefer (see Figure 2.3). Many teachers list topics that are consistent with materials, or they might identify a unit by the name of a novel or a project. No judgment on this part; it just gives direction to the next step for distributing the standards.

Once in a while teachers may say they want to change the sequence or the topics to match new materials, or a new teacher may want to create a new

---

FIGURE 2.3
Sample Unit Titles

Grade 4 History of the United States: Revolution to Reconstruction
    Unit 1: The War for Independence (1700s–1780s)
    Unit 2: Creating a New Government (1781–1789)
    Unit 3: Building the New Nation (1790–1830)
    Unit 4: The Growth of the Republic (1800s–1850)
    Unit 5: The United States Prior to the Civil War (1820s–1861)
    Unit 6: The Civil War and Reconstruction (1861–1870s)

Grade 9 Science: Living Environment
    Unit 1: Cell Structure and Function
    Unit 2: Cells and Energy
    Unit 3: Plant Diversity
    Unit 4: Plant Structure and Function
    Unit 5: Human Systems and Homeostasis
    Unit 6: Nervous and Endocrine Systems

Adapted from the Tennessee Department of Education, 2016, and from the New York State Education Department, 2016.

sequence. Not a problem. We suggest that teachers use the most likely unit titles for the coming school year.

3. The Pacing Matrix (optional)

With the course document prepped and ready for use, a teacher can now create the scope and sequence of the course. Since most standards documents are written for a year or a semester, the teacher will want to first sequence the standards, or distribute them, into reporting periods or unit titles. Distributing standards by reporting period is the way to ensure that all standards are taught and assessed, even at the elementary level. The matrix is an optional step but a great idea for any highly procedural classes such as reading in the early elementary years or mathematics throughout all grade levels (see Figures 2.4 and 2.5). But note that it is also an extra step that requires creating a second document with the quarter or unit columns on the right side.

FIGURE 2.4
Standards Distribution Matrix for English in Grade 9

English 9 Matrix	Q1	Q2	Q3	Q4
RL.1. Cite strong and thorough textual evidence to support analysis of what the text says explicitly as well as inferences drawn from the text.		X		
RL.2. Determine a theme or central idea of a text and analyze in detail its development over the course of the text, including how it emerges and is shaped and refined by specific details; provide an objective summary of the text.	X			
RL.3. Analyze how complex characters (e.g., those with multiple or conflicting motivations) develop over the course of a text, interact with other characters, and advance the plot or develop the theme.	X			

Adapted from Common Core State Standards, 2010a.

A matrix is a helpful visual tool that can organize sorting standards into reporting periods or into the unit titles mentioned above. A simple spreadsheet will do the trick. For example, a yearlong English language arts course has about 54 standards. Those 54 standards can be copied and pasted from the course document into the first column of a spreadsheet with only minor

FIGURE 2.5

Standards Distribution Matrix for Mathematics in Grade 1

Mathematics 1st Grade	T1	T2	T3
1.OA.1. Use addition and subtraction within 20 to solve word problems involving situations of adding to, taking from, putting together, taking apart, and comparing, with unknowns in all positions, such as by using objects, drawings, and equations with a symbol for the unknown number to represent the problem.		X	
1.OA.2. Solve word problems that call for addition of three whole numbers whose sum is less than or equal to 20, for example, by using objects, drawings, and equations with a symbol for the unknown number to represent the problem.			X
1.OA.3. Apply properties of operations as strategies to add and subtract. [Students need not use formal terms for these properties.] Examples: If $8 + 3 = 11$ is known, then $3 + 8 = 11$ is also known. (Commutative property of addition.) To add $2 + 6 + 4$, the second two numbers can be added to make a ten, so $2 + 6 + 4 = 2 + 10 = 12$. (Associative property of addition.)		X	
1.OA.4. Understand subtraction as an unknown-addend problem. For example, subtract $10 - 8$ by finding the number that makes 10 when added to 8.			X

Adapted from Common Core State Standards, 2010b.

adjustments. The next two to four column headings reflect the reporting period breakdown, such as Quarter 1, Quarter 2, Quarter 3, and Quarter 4. The teacher then reads each standard and marks the cell corresponding to the reporting period when it will be taught and assessed.

Although a matrix is really only useful for subjects like English or the arts, where the standards are not always sequential and sometimes need to be revisited, some schools use the matrix process as a way to guide reading and discussing the standards. Having teachers who teach the same course, such as a team of 4th grade teachers or the 8th grade and high school algebra teachers, work together to distribute standards helps to increase consistency in course content and curriculum pacing. For subjects such as science or social studies that tend to be topic based and whose standards are listed in that manner, the matrix may be unnecessary. In some areas such as history, the matrix is useful for distributing the historical practices, as they tend to be a longer list of about 20–30 skills.

4. The Standards Distributed by Reporting Period

Once completed, the matrix spreadsheet can then group the standards by reporting periods. That way the teachers can easily view the standards they will teach to and report on by quarters, trimesters, or however their classes are organized. We consider the matrix a worksheet and not a required document in the curriculum files.

Now with the original document on the screen and the matrix printed, the teacher can create the curriculum files. The teacher opens the original course document and saves it under a new name, such as 6 Math Quarter 1. She then uses the "deleting secret" to delete all standards that are not taught in Quarter 1. Using the original course document again, she saves Quarter 2, then Quarter 3, and Quarter 4, repeating the deleting process. This deleting process reduces error and is more productive than cutting and pasting or retyping standards into boxes or columns. It saves teachers a lot of time.

Now the teacher has the overall course document, the year at a glance, and all of the standards distributed by reporting period.

5. The Unit Plans

Once the standards are distributed into reporting periods (approximately 9 weeks for a quarter, 12 weeks for a trimester, and 18 weeks for a semester), the teacher can then further distribute them into smaller units of two to four weeks within the term. Now that it has been determined what will be taught and assessed within each reporting period, the teacher further distributes the standards into logical groups of units that last two to four weeks within the term. Similar to the process described above, the teacher uses either the original course document or the reporting period document to individually save by the unit titles and then deletes the standards not intended to be taught in that unit.

It is important to acknowledge that some standards may show up in more than one unit and, along the same lines, it is really important not to overpopulate units with too many standards. A good rule of thumb is that a standard is included in a unit *only* if it is being taught and assessed in the unit. It can be understood that standards will be "used" throughout the year once they are taught.

Now the teacher has an original standards document, standards distributed by reporting periods, and standards distributed by unit titles. Similar to the overall standards document, teachers may write a sentence or two to describe the unit and add the time recommended to complete it. We are not finished with the unit documents, sometimes referred to as one-pagers because they should not exceed a double-sided printed sheet. See Figure 2.6.

There are three more parts to the unit plan:

- **Clarify the standards and unpack them to each specific lesson**, preparing for lesson instruction and scoring student performance to the standards.
- **Locate, design, and briefly describe summative and formative assessment**, ensuring direct alignment to the standards. Include assessments, labs, or projects that integrate critical and creative thinking skills.
- **Gather and study resources about the content and skills of the unit**, including a primary resource, such as the selected text for the course, and supplemental materials, such as online applications, to ensure complete understanding of what is to be learned and to gain ideas for unit and lesson activities.

Since the reporting documents might define summative assessments, the unit document may need to show some formative assessments, chapter or unit tests, and common assessments briefly noted in the assessment section. Although it is frequently touted that assessment drives instruction, it is critical to remember that the curriculum standards drive the assessment and the instruction. Many teachers say they feel stymied by having to design assessments before they have perused materials or started drafting some instructional activities; others are comfortable designing assessments first. Similarly, teachers may want to list some of the resources that are available for the unit. When teachers curate these documents in online folders, many of the resources are linked to files in the same folder.

With this unit planning document prepared and saved in a shared online repository, it is now ready for the teacher or team of teachers to access and reference when developing lesson plans for the upcoming week's learning sessions. This process incorporates the daily classroom lessons and assessments, and we'll look more closely at these elements in later chapters. For teachers to work effectively—and work together—on curriculum development, they must have reliable access to school computers. Unlimited shared access within and across grade levels to an electronic folder system allows teachers to discuss student performance based on the curriculum using a streamlined and uncomplicated procedure.

Now the teacher has an original standards document, standards distributed by reporting period, and a number of unit one-pagers that show the standards for each two- to four-week unit with brief references to assessments and

FIGURE 2.6

Unit Document for Unit 4 in Mathematics in Grade 6

SCHOOL LOGO

MATHEMATICS 6
Middle School Division - Grade 6
Unit 4: <<insert unit title>>
<<insert unit length>>

Unit Description

<<Enter a description, which may include essential questions and enduring understandings.>>

Standards

6.G.1. Find the area of right triangles, other triangles, special quadrilaterals, and polygons by composing into rectangles or decomposing into triangles and other shapes; apply these techniques in the context of solving real-world and mathematical problems.

6.G.2. Find the volume of a right rectangular prism with fractional edge lengths by packing it with unit cubes of the appropriate unit fraction edge lengths, and show that the volume is the same as would be found by multiplying the edge lengths of the prism. Apply the formulas V = lwh and V = bh to find volumes of right rectangular prisms with fractional edge lengths in the context of solving real-world and mathematical problems.

6.G.3. Draw polygons in the coordinate plane given coordinates for the vertices; use coordinates to find the length of a side joining points with the same first coordinate or the same second coordinate. Apply these techniques in the context of solving real-world and mathematical problems.

6.G.4. Represent three-dimensional figures using nets made up of rectangles and triangles, and use the nets to find the surface area of these figures. Apply these techniques in the context of solving real-world and mathematical problems.

6.SP.1. Recognize a statistical question as one that anticipates variability in the data related to the question and accounts for it in the answers. For example, "How old am I?" is not a statistical question, but "How old are the students in my school?" is a statistical question because one anticipates variability in students' ages.

Assessment

<<List the common, agreed-upon assessment(s) of unit, which tend to be summative but can include formative.>>

Resources

<<List the resources of the unit, which can include primary textbook and also supplementary resources.>>

Adapted from Common Core State Standards, 2010b.

resources. A teacher can save a copy of the unit document onto his computer and begin to write lessons on that file using his preferred template or format for planning. The system's simplicity is key; most teachers can quickly learn how to access folders and select the curriculum folder, the grade-level folder, or the unit planner document in order to begin designing lessons.

An Important Note About Unit and Lesson Planning

Chapter 3 is devoted to the next phase of curriculum writing, lesson planning and delivery, which translates the unit into action. Because one of the most frequently asked questions in unit and lesson planning has to do with how the daily objective needs to be written, we decided to address it as a separate issue here. As you will see, the goal of the lesson is critical because it is how students self-assess. It is important to consider the specificity needed when unpacking standards to lesson objectives, sometimes called goals or learning intentions, and how the type of knowledge (declarative or procedural) addressed in the lesson is best learned.

"Just-Right" Lesson Goals

Writing daily learning objectives is not new to any teacher. Ever since Madeline Hunter suggested that teachers "set an objective," teachers have busily tried to find the perfect way to write active learning objectives. Most standards are too broadly written for daily lessons, and thus the teacher needs to unpack goals from grade-level or course standards in a curriculum. Although one grade-level or course standard may last over a few days, the specific learning goals should vary from lesson to lesson.

Elementary teachers have learned to unpack the standard into "I can" statements to make the content more accessible to the students. This language lends itself to knowledge that is procedural, such as learning and practicing steps in a process. We recommend that teachers also use the phrase "I know" because some content needs to be learned as information, or declarative knowledge. Here are some examples:

An elementary Arkansas standard for social studies:

Standard: Know the role of citizens and governments in carrying out constitutional principles for the common good.

- I know the roles of the local, state, and federal governments.
- I know how governments bring about change for a group of people.
- I can make a plan to take action for my community.

A grade 6 New York math standard:

Standard: Understand solving an equation or inequality as a process of answering a question: Which values from a specified set, if any, make the equation or inequality true? Use substitution to determine whether a given number in a specified set makes an equation or inequality true.

- Determine if a number sentence is true or false based on the given symbol.
- Know the definition of a solution in the context of substituting a value for a variable to see if it makes the equation true.
- Use substitution to determine whether a given number in a specified set makes an equation or inequality true.

A secondary standard for science adapted from Next Generation Science Standards:

Standard: Demonstrate that atoms, and mass, are conserved during a chemical reaction by balancing chemical equations.

- Know the law of conservation of mass.
- Balance chemical equations.

A grade 9–10 English standard from the Missouri Expectations:

Standard: Using appropriate text, determine two or more themes, analyze their development throughout the text, and relate the themes to life experiences; provide an objective and concise summary of the text.

- Find themes in the text.
- Analyze the development of two or more themes across the text.
- Know how the themes relate to the context of history and to situations today.
- Summarize the text, including specific references to the themes.

In *Standards-Based Learning in Action: Moving from Theory to Practice,* Schimmer, Hillman, and Stalets (2018) explain additional ways to unpack standards into just-right lesson goals. The know, understand, and do (KUD) method "break[s] down standards into categories of knowledge, overarching understandings, and skills" (p. 38). Another approach the authors suggest is for teachers to analyze the benchmarks or statements found within sets of standards, such as from a state or national association, as some of the language can lend itself or easily be adapted to serve as lesson objectives. Often state mathematics standards, particularly in the early elementary grades, are written in a way that one could easily unpack into lesson goals. A final suggestion they have is for teachers to employ an approach described by Dimich Vagle, where teachers organize "*I can* statements into learning goals ladders to show learning progression, from the emerging stages to standard fulfillment" (p. 41). Using a visual, the actual shape of a ladder, with each lesson goal as a rung culminating in the standard reflected at the top, can be useful when building just-right targets for subjects like English and social studies.

It is important for the teacher to be mindful of the following: not only does the just-right lesson goal drive instructional planning and assessment selection, but it is the essential ingredient for effective feedback for students. For that reason, it is important to provide the objectives in clear, brief, and measurable statements that directly align back to the standards. Unpacking standards into learning goals during the unit planning stage saves teachers a lot of time to study the subject-area goals and write or modify lessons. The lesson schema, as we will see in the next chapter, will depend on students' ability to write the goal and self-score as well as the teacher's ability to monitor progress.

Declarative and Procedural Knowledge

Learning and processing new information looks different depending on whether a student retains the knowledge as declarative or procedural memory. Declarative knowledge is factual or conceptual, such as learning about animal adaptations in science; it is easy to learn and easy to forget. Procedural knowledge typically involves learning and practicing steps, such as drawing two-point perspective in visual art; it is hard to learn but also hard to forget once it is practiced to automaticity. Although teachers intuitively know the difference between declarative knowledge (content) and procedural knowledge (skill), it's only recently that we have considered the value of identifying standards and objectives as declarative and procedural in curriculum documents. Cueing the teacher about the distinction helps him plan activities for either thinking skills or for practice.

In a curriculum document, the statements of declarative knowledge (facts, concepts, generalizations, and principles) can be prefaced by the words *understands* or *knows*. The following examples demonstrate how this works for science, math, and geography statements:

The student

- Knows the effect of balanced and unbalanced forces on an object's motion (science).
- Understands measures of central tendency, frequency, and distribution with rational numbers (math).

- Knows the ways people take aspects of the environment into account when deciding on locations for human activities (geography).

In each example, the word *knows* or *understands* indicates declarative concepts and also provides the technical cue for the teacher to plan to use the verb ladder to determine the level of instruction and activity expected by the students. The verb ladder refers to the progression from low-level verbs, such as *identify* or *describe,* up to the higher-level verbs, such as *analyze* or *synthesize,* which signal most of us to design lessons to "move up on Bloom's taxonomy." Teachers who use this format can read the declarative statement and decide for themselves which verb to use or, in other words, whether to have the students identify, describe, explain, solve a problem, compare, analyze, or apply information in a new situation. Using the verb ladder approach, the standards are the agreed-upon concepts or principles about the content, but the teacher has the flexibility to decide on the level of activity at the lesson design stage (see Chapter 3). This approach is different from previous curriculum design formats, which directed teachers to write the objective statements with a presumption of activity, thereby limiting students to performing a very particular exercise designated by the verb at the beginning of the objective statement.

Veteran teachers may remember the days of behavioral objective writing and the admonition that understanding cannot be assessed. Behavioral objectives were suggested in the 1960s before the neurological confirmation by most scientists that we learn declarative and procedural knowledge differently. But in the verb ladder, *understands* and *knows* both serve as placeholders for active verbs, which translate into activities and experiences that help students organize declarative knowledge. If, however, the standard addresses procedural knowledge, the statement of student learning should begin with a verb that describes the steps that need to be practiced to attain automaticity, such as *add, compose, sing, draw,* or *graph.*

This simple distinction is critical because it enables a teacher to scan curriculum documents and gauge immediately which standards will require students to organize facts and information before they use thinking skills (i.e., declarative statements that begin with *understands* or *knows*) and which standards will require tasks that involve extended repetition or practice (i.e., procedural statements that begin with other verbs), as seen in Figure 2.7. The next two chapters on instruction and assessment will explain the importance of the issue in practice.

FIGURE 2.7
Impact of Knowledge Type on Lesson Planning

Declarative knowledge: What we know	Procedural knowledge: How we do it
• The goal is to *understand* or *know* the content. • It entails gathering and organizing factual and conceptual information. • Students use the 12 thinking skills to apply new information to generate new ideas. • Examples include events in history, plants and animals, or website designs.	• The goal states the procedure with words such as *writes, solves, sings,* or *designs.* • The teacher models the steps of the procedure. • It involves following steps and practicing to automaticity. • Examples include writing a story, solving equations, drawing a portrait, or serving a volleyball.

A Formula for Success

Before we dive deep into Chapter 3 and high-quality lesson planning, it is important to pause briefly and consider how the timeline for and steps found within the curriculum development process are affected by shifting to this form for curriculum writing. How can we guarantee that these foundational documents will be sought after by new and veteran teachers for daily planning purposes? In other words, how can Belinda permanently remove the roadblocks that existed between curriculum documents and teachers' regular use of them?

Historically, curriculum development took place over a seven-year cycle that emphasized a different subject area each year. During year 1, the study year, teachers in a subject area would convene a committee to study the changes in the field. During year 2, they would pilot any significant changes, which generally translated to using new textbooks in some classrooms. The committee would officially adopt new materials in year 3, use the materials for the next few years, and finally, in the last year of the cycle, fill out evaluations recommending changes for the next cycle. Essentially, this process supported purchasing textbooks more than anything else; it was mostly a budgetary issue, in other words. The seven-year cycle allowed the time to rotate through subject areas in order to spread the cost of purchasing materials over several years. In many schools, the cycle eventually was shortened to five years, mainly to accommodate the technology or computer literacy changes of the 1980s and 1990s.

Since the turn of the century, an exponentially increasing amount of curriculum resources, including online options and print textbooks, are designed to readily align with learning standards; an infinite amount of pertinent instructional materials and research can also be easily accessed online. In return, the curriculum development cycle of today can have greater flexibility and be more expeditiously executed than in years past, with the course documents and unit plans in a form that entices regular use. The formula for success then includes two complementary components: (1) a renewal framework for a subject area in which significant changes are being considered and (2) an annual housekeeping plan to ensure no subject area becomes outdated due to various factors, such as the curriculum area that is under review monopolizing attention and time, which risks the unintentional neglect of others (see Figure 2.8). Let's take a look at how these two components can work in harmony.

FIGURE 2.8
Sample Timeline for Annual Curriculum Housekeeping Tasks

Quarter 1	Quarter 2	Quarter 3	Quarter 4
Teach unit 1. Review unit 1.	Teach unit 3. Review unit 3.	Teach unit 6. Review unit 6.	Teach unit 8. Review unit 8.
Teach unit 2. Review unit 2.	Teach unit 4. Review unit 4.	Teach unit 7. Review unit 7.	Teach unit 9. Review unit 9.
Analyze past and upcoming standards, and make adjustments as needed.	Teach unit 5. Review unit 5. Analyze past and upcoming standards, and make adjustments as needed.	Analyze past and upcoming standards, and make adjustments as needed. Vet the course description for the upcoming year, and make adjustments as needed.	Analyze past and upcoming standards, and make adjustments as needed.

If we were starting a school from scratch or preparing a brand new course and developing its curriculum from the ground up, we would suggest that the curriculum writing process outlined in this chapter be followed: prepare the course document, outline the prescribed content, and begin to plan for units of learning that can be readily accessed for lesson planning. Once the curriculum for courses within each subject area is established, the following annual housekeeping tasks should be completed:

1. Examine each unit for potential changes in the future delivery of the unit, such as adjustments to content breadth or depth, instructional approach, learning activities, and assessment techniques.
2. Analyze the scope and sequence of the prescribed content by unit and reporting period to make shifts in pacing, if deemed necessary.
3. Review the course description prior to each time the course is taught to ensure it accurately reflects the offering.

It is suggested these tasks be completed in the order listed above, which is the reverse order of how the curriculum was originally designed, as examination of individual units helps to inform pacing decisions, which ultimately supports the confirmation or revision of the course description. Equally important, it is advised that a review of each individual unit immediately follow its delivery to ensure needed adjustments are not forgotten or inadvertently overlooked. Course descriptions many times need to be published for the next school year prior to the end of the current school year, which means that sometimes up to a whole semester of curriculum has not been delivered prior to preparations for it to be offered again, so having an opportunity to review at least half or more of the year's content can provide at least some direction for the soon-to-be-published course description.

It is most likely that you, the reader, are a teacher, principal, or curriculum director who works in a school with some sort of curriculum already in place and are looking for an entry point into either introducing or further developing a curriculum based on well-articulated learning goals. In determining how to begin the process, conducting an audit or a needs assessment can identify curricular areas or courses with the greatest need so you can address those first for renewal purposes. Examples of greatest need would include subject areas or courses that do not have or are not using an identified set of standards, offerings in need of updates due to changes in the field, outdated textbooks or software that are a top priority for replacement, or a new course that will be taught in the near future.

Summary

Benjamin Bloom and the assessment professors were right. Teachers have a better chance of guiding students toward success when the curriculum standards are spiraled by levels and accessible both in format and language. Whether a first-time teacher or a teacher changing a grade level or a course, it is helpful to make sure that the curriculum is a guide for instruction and assessment. The guide should include standards, pacing, and possibly recommendations for assessments and resources. A teacher should be able to use the guide to develop her own lesson plans.

Using the formatting recommendations in this chapter, teachers will have the autonomy to plan lessons, choose resources, and vary the activities and assessments. The next chapter addresses planning and delivery of instruction. Specifically, it introduces a lesson planning format that guides teachers to improve student learning using research-based strategies.

Teacher Voice

Belinda Parini, *Physical Education and Health Teacher in Melbourne, Australia*

I began my teaching career as a physical education (PE) and health teacher in 2005. Over my career, I've had the privilege of teaching students from years 7 to 12, all from diverse ethnic backgrounds and learning abilities. I've held numerous roles in the school I've spent most of my career, a government secondary school in the western suburbs of Melbourne, Victoria, Australia, and it would be remiss of me not to mention the experiences gained in my year spent abroad teaching in the United Kingdom. After 10 years focusing solely on what I could do as an individual teacher to improve the learning outcomes of my students, my biggest challenge presented itself when I found myself in the role of the school's curriculum leader. Moving from serving as a PE teacher in charge of the curriculum carried out within her own classroom to being tasked with ensuring a viable curriculum existed and is in use by all teachers in all departments for all students within the school sure did bring its challenges.

I think back to six months earlier when, as the head for the PE department, I was first introduced to the Big Four. The concept of teaching, assessing, and recordkeeping to the standards set off an array of questions I began asking myself:

- Why is it that in the eight years I had been at this school we made very few changes to the curriculum we taught, the assessment tasks we used, and the way we reported back to parents?
- Why was I leading a department that had quite frankly never really examined whether or not what we were doing was working for *all* students?
- Were we simply teaching a curriculum that we had been given by our predecessors and minimal changes were made because the tasks seemed

to be effective and we had the assumption for most of the students that learning was taking place?

We seemed to be able to justify when students did not perform as well as others, so we did not question ourselves, our practices, or the curriculum employed.

Fast-forward six months to an initial conversation I had as the curriculum leader with subject-area department heads, I asked each of them who served as Key Learning Area (KLA) leaders in their department to share with me their curriculum documents. Upon reviewing them, a pattern began to emerge. As a team, we were missing a critical piece, the proverbial "big picture," which is what students should know and be able to do by the end of each course. Without the first tenet of the Big Four, it had shown and would continue to be difficult to focus on changes to instruction, assessment, reporting, and feedback without identifying the learning standards or goals for each course.

In addition, our documents showed that there were inconsistencies in our curriculum with terms that identified different types of initiatives over the years, scope and sequences that were started but not completed, and lots of assessment headers that did not include necessary descriptions of tasks. Our team agreed that not one of the documents looked easy to interpret. I was concerned that improving learning for all students would be nearly impossible without having curriculum documents that teachers could effectively use to plan their delivery. And that moment initiated our journey into developing a well-articulated, guaranteed, and viable standards-based curriculum consistent across all subject areas that addresses state-wide learning targets and ultimately improves learning for each student.

From facilitating curriculum development, I've had many "light-bulb" moments. One of these moments occurred when I was reviewing the detailed year 11 and 12 courses of students provided to us by state writing teams, similar to Advanced Placement (AP) or International Baccalaureate (IB) curriculums. For us, we found these detailed descriptions of learning targets to be incredibly helpful in knowing what students should know and be able to do by the end of the course. Why didn't we have these learning targets identified for our junior curriculums in years 7–10? There is no secret to the fact that our school, and probably many others, has dramatically improved students' results in their final year of schooling. It's been a process that has led to a rigorous, well-planned and -delivered curriculum that aligns to the standards and is assessed to the standards. It was shocking to realize that this level of rigor was not always evident in our junior curriculum.

So, the seed was planted, first with curriculum leaders like me and then among the teaching staff. We decided to dedicate time and resources to the development of learning targets. The school dedicated planning time on curriculum days and professional development sessions for teachers to work on these documents and ensured that all teachers could easily access organized files on a shared drive so they could provide suggestions, feedback, and critique. We used the process described by the Big Four whereby you start with a standards document, and that initiates the "deleting" process to create multiple documents.

While time is the precious commodity that teachers often state that they lack, investing time into planning has been critical in seeing the success of the work that has been completed thus far. This work has given our staff a process for shifting focus from how to improve teaching to how to improve student learning. After our initial work on improving our curriculum documents, we began to see gains in overall student achievement. Including teachers in this work ensured they had a voice and that curriculum leaders were listening; they also shared that they believed the process provided greater clarity of what was to be taught, which naturally extended to students and what students were expected to learn.

With the flexibility and diversity of modern technology, it won't be long until these documents will not only be accessible but could also be widely read by parents and the wider community. How effective will reporting to parents be when a clear process on building a standards-based curriculum is documented. But ultimately what's more important is that teachers no longer have to keep reinventing the wheel when planning is concerned and instead can focus on the sole purpose behind the word *teacher*.

For some teachers, the big concern was autonomy and feeling like the standards might be rigid. Much like the year 11 and 12 study designs or the AP and IB curriculums, the standards are generally conceptual or skill-based, so they provide the breadth of the content, not the required specifics. In addition, teachers still design their own lessons and assessments. In some cases, grade levels or departments agree to some common assessments, but that generally both saves teacher time and provides some cross-subject data for curriculum improvements.

When the curriculum has been planned, it allows for engaging, meaningful, and insightful ways to teach, which ultimately leads to the reason we all became teachers in the first place: not only to see student learning and achievement but, more important, to be witness to the growth of self-regulated thinkers and learners in the classroom and beyond. So, my advice? Start working on your documents.

Lesson Planning, Delivery, and What the Students Do

Jennifer Collins wrote about being a first-year teacher a number of years ago, "I was so excited to meet my students and help them learn; however, I was not aware of the difficulties that lay ahead. As a college student, lesson planning was easy. I was told, 'Pick a standard from any subject and create a lesson.' It was creative and we could follow any format we wanted to use. The college professors encouraged student engagement, so my lessons involved students spending most of the class periods doing activities. My assignments were always enjoyable because, of course, I selected the most exciting standards for that particular grade level. I could plan for hours, crafting the perfect lesson for a few of the most interesting standards. My high marks for lesson plans gave me a lot of confidence, so I started my teaching career with the idea that planning would be a breeze. Teaching would be fun."

Tyler Jones remembered lesson planning when he was at university as a difficult task due to the amount of detail he was required to include to show his understanding of what both he and the students would do in a class. He said that the planning required by his professors was comprehensive. They had a complex template that required filling in many sections ranging from all of the applicable standards, assessments for and of learning, differentiation for groups of students, examples of technology use, and reflection on the lesson after delivery. He said that designing daily lessons with such thoroughness would be impossible to do for five classes a day. When pressed to explain how he did plan once he started teaching, Tyler explained the activity planning technique he learned during student teaching. "We would start by planning the activity for students to do, organize the necessary resources, and then find standards that seemed to go with the activities." He explained, "The teachers told us to try to make sure there were a lot of 'hands on' activities to keep students active and engaged."

Daily Lesson Planning

When Jennifer and Tyler started teaching, they asked many experienced classroom teachers for advice about lesson planning. "I think I plan the activities for the unit, but I don't really plan lessons *per se*" was a response Tyler heard from a teacher in his school. Teachers said that they planned activities for a couple of weeks out, but since things changed every day, they might not actually be at the exact point they thought they would be when they wrote the plans. That prompted these kinds of answers: "I've been teaching for a long time, so I don't really have to plan daily lessons anymore." "I make slides for the content I need to teach, and others are the directions for student activities." "I look at where the students are each day and take them to the next step." Teachers said that one of the biggest problems with planning had to do with covering the content or staying on the pacing calendar, so most of them did not describe planning as a day-to-day, bell-to-bell task. More than likely, they had unit plans with standards, a series of assessments, and a list of learning activities that were not necessarily sequenced or paced.

Despite what some teachers might say, they do prepare plenty of lessons. In fact, each teacher plans anywhere from 500 to 800 lessons a year depending on their subject and grade level. Something interesting we noticed when observing classes was that most teachers follow a strikingly similar classroom teaching routine. Almost every teacher has an objective written on the board whether or not she addresses it explicitly; then, she asks a question, some calling it a "hook," intending to engage all of the students. Usually only two or three students answer, and the teacher begins to teach for about 10–20 minutes, demonstrate something, or explain the directions for an activity. Depending on the time frame, the teacher assigns a classroom task and then walks around guiding some students and leaving others to work independently for another 10–20 minutes. In almost every class, the bell rings too soon, and elementary students collect belongings to put in cubbies and the secondary school students are reminded to finish assignments for homework. These recognizable steps to delivering daily lessons likely originated with Madeline C. Hunter's *Mastery Teaching* (1982) schema. Even new teachers tell us they learned a variation of this teaching model in recent university classes.

Seeing the ubiquitous teaching model led us to identify it as pedagogical automaticity. Pedagogy is the study of teaching. Automaticity implies that a performance can be carried out as a habit without thinking about the steps, like driving a car or brushing your teeth. It also implies flexibility and the ability to shape it for yourself. Pedagogical automaticity refers to the habits that teachers learn over the years. University courses provide opportunities for aspiring teachers to develop effective habits of daily lesson planning and teaching, as shared by Jennifer and Tyler. But our experiences and interactions with teachers have also shown us that teachers—new to and veterans of the profession—say they learned to teach by watching their own teachers in school.

Preschool through 12th grade schooling is comprised of anywhere between 10,000 to 15,000 hours in which students have observed teaching and experienced firsthand how most daily lessons should progress. This prior experience with and upbringing in the field of education as a student before becoming a teacher is a remarkable and unique trait of our profession. In fact, it provides context for how a new teacher and a veteran teacher can be given a similar teaching assignment since both tend to have pedagogical automaticity. How does this set of teaching habits, this pedagogical automaticity, develop and why did we find it useful for the Big Four discussion?

Let's dig deeper. If we are looking to improve every child's learning, we should consider how teaching habits from previous generations positively influenced lesson planning and delivery. Rather than making dramatic changes, we needed to determine how newer findings in neuroscience and research have evolved our understanding of learning. What adjustments or refinements needed to be made in light of this new information? Also, although we inherited our pedagogical automaticity primarily from the teachers we had in elementary and secondary school, we learned the routines but were not necessarily aware of how well all students in class performed. Yes, think of the grading curve. It may be that part of our pedagogical automaticity contributes to a large number of students successfully performing in all classes, but it *inadvertently* accepts that there will always be some students who will not perform well in any given class from primary to secondary classrooms, from math to music.

If that is the case, we should make a few adjustments to our lesson planning and delivery. So how do we know what needs to change? To find out, let's revisit a brief history of lesson planning.

A Brief History of Lesson Planning

There are many examples in the literature, but one interesting schema was developed by Johann F. Herbart (1776–1841), a German philosopher (Ornstein & Levine, 1987). Herbart and his followers advocated planning to help the teacher guide students through the academic process of acquiring knowledge. He suggested five instructional steps for each lesson:

1. *Prepare.* The teacher refers to materials learned earlier to stimulate the learner.
2. *Present.* The teacher presents new information to the students.
3. *Associate.* The teacher deliberately relates the new information to previously learned materials.
4. *Systematize.* The teacher gives examples of the generalizations or the principles to be learned by the students.
5. *Apply.* The students try the new materials or new ideas to demonstrate their personal mastery of knowledge.

The schema sounds very similar to what we do today. Herbart's schema encouraged teachers to plan to deliver direct instruction using the steps described; the assumption was that every teacher could learn to follow the steps daily while working on the overarching curriculum over the long term. This sounds very similar to a spiraled curriculum in which, over time, students would continuously add to previous learnings (Cooney, Cross, & Trunk, 1993). So, lesson planning has been around for a long time, and it is not surprising to find the vestiges of Herbart's work in contemporary lesson planning techniques.

Whether teaching in one-room schoolhouses with multilevel students, for after-school mandolin lessons, or in a remote learning environment, teachers learn quickly that planning lessons allows them to keep order in the classroom as well as stay on pace with the curriculum. Many more leading educators would propose planning and delivering instruction guided by a series of daily steps as well.

Events of Instruction

Robert Gagne (1965) proposed nine instruction "events" similar in concept to the Herbartian steps, but he added specific guidance for assessment:

1. Gain learners' attention.
2. Inform learners of the lesson objective.
3. Stimulate recall of previous learning.

4. Present stimulus material.
5. Provide learning guidance.
6. Elicit performance (i.e., practice).
7. Provide feedback.
8. Assess performance.
9. Enhance retention and transfer.

Similar to Herbart's, the schema expanded the steps with more attention to student performance.

The Workshop Model

In the 1980s, Donald Graves suggested teaching writing through the workshop model, specifically addressing how much time to spend in each segment. Teachers were encouraged to have the following routine for each lesson:

1. Mini-lesson (20 percent of the lesson time)
2. Independent work time (60 percent of lesson time)
3. Share session (20 percent of the lesson time)

The mini-lesson is an important part of the lesson because it allows the teacher to instruct the whole class on the teaching point for the day. Once students experience direct instruction through teacher modeling and guiding practice, they practice as they work alone, in pairs, or in small groups with the teacher during independent work time. That gives the teacher time to check in to assess or reteach, if necessary. The workshop session ends with a share session, during which the teacher highlights several students' work as it relates to the mini-lesson goal and recaps the learning. Many teachers recognize the workshop model as gradual release of responsibility, which intends to transfer mastery of skills from the teacher to the student (Duke & Pearson, 2002; Pearson & Gallagher, 1983).

The workshop and gradual release of responsibility models are designed primarily for teaching literacy skills, such as reading and writing. As we noted in earlier chapters, reading and writing are taught initially as procedural knowledge, so the lesson schema requires practice for students to reproduce the skills. Not surprisingly, many math teachers have adopted a variation on the models, naming the steps *I do, we do, you do*. These models work well for teaching procedural content, but they are not as useful for highly declarative topics, as one might find in the areas of science, history, health, and music theory.

Hunter's Teaching Schema for Mastery Teaching

Probably the most practiced lesson delivery method is by Madeline C. Hunter, still taught today in many universities. Published in her book *Mastery Teaching* (1982), Hunter recommended these steps:

1. *Set the objective.* The teacher identifies what the students will learn that class period.
2. *Anticipatory set.* The teacher uses a "hook" to engage students' attention.
3. *Input and modeling.* The teacher presents information in the form of a lecture, demonstration, or readings. The teacher presents a successful example of the product of the lesson.
4. *Checking for understanding and guided practice.* The teacher checks the students to make sure that they are getting it. The teacher observes the students demonstrating their new learning and provides feedback.
5. *Independent practice.* Each student applies the information related to the objective.
6. *Closure.* The teacher summarizes the learning of the lesson.

Hunter's schema stuck. It was a short series of steps that teachers could follow, practice, and use every day, every lesson; the routine became the pedagogical automaticity. As one teacher told us, "I can cover any class for another teacher because I have a tried and true routine."

It is also important to note that many principals learned to supervise classroom teaching by checking for the parts of a Hunter lesson as the touchstones of accountability. By using the schema, each teacher had the promise of becoming a master teacher. For decades, then, teachers would learn to plan and deliver lessons this way, and principals would evaluate teaching using the steps as the quintessential elements of good instruction. It became the pedagogical automaticity for most teachers from the 1980s to the present day.

It still left us with a question about unit planning, daily lesson planning, lessons lasting many more days than planned, and not all students performing well. Units seemed to have standards, but daily lessons needed them unpacked to specify what about the standard would be taught that day. We hypothesized that if teachers did not unpack the standards to specify what would be taught and learned for daily lessons, but instead planned activities, then that seemed to leave too much room for "wraparound lessons," or lessons that were planned for one day and continued for a few more. Remember that was one of teachers' frustrations—staying on the pacing calendar or covering the content. It seemed that the daily schema might be the most promising tool to adjust.

GANAG: A Teaching Schema for Master Learners

When we talk with teachers and principals, they tell us that the Hunter delivery model works. But, when we ask teachers if it works for all students, they hesitate. It seems that every classroom teacher, from primary to secondary, recognizes that a few students in every class disengage to the point that it affects their overall learning. Those are the students, teachers tell us, who end up with lower grades. If the model works for most students but not all students, then we thought it would be worth studying what could be changed about it to improve learning but not require major changes for teachers, because we acknowledge how difficult it is to change habits.

Some noteworthy events happened since the 1980s when Hunter's model became popular. The first is the dramatic shift in research from behaviorism to neuroscience. With the invention of MRI (magnetic resonance imaging) testing and other equipment, our understanding about how humans make memories, or in other words, how humans learn, changed. By most accounts, we are still in the beginning stages of knowing how people learn, but one crucial development confirms that humans learn declarative and procedural knowledge very differently. We updated Hunter's schema to include that element, allowing teachers to determine whether lessons would focus on procedural knowledge (need to practice) or declarative knowledge (need to use critical and creative thinking skills).

Second was the publication of Marzano, Pickering, and Pollock's *Classroom Instruction That Works,* in 2001. (In 2012, ASCD published a second corroborating edition.) With access to so many studies, Jane and her colleagues found research-based strategies they referred to as nine high-yield strategies. *High-yield strategy* refers to the probability that using the technique would help one retain knowledge better. Since many students have difficulty engaging for long periods of time and therefore do not retain the needed information, these strategies could prove useful if students learned how to use them during day-to-day instruction. This would, by design, make lessons more student-centered.

These nine are *learning strategies*; they are referred to as instructional strategies because teachers can teach and provide opportunities for students to use them to retain information in class.

1. Identify similarities and differences.
2. Summarize and take notes.
3. Recognize effort and provide recognition.
4. Provide homework and practice.
5. Use nonlinguistic representations.

6. Use cooperative learning.
7. Set objectives and provide feedback.
8. Generate and test hypotheses.
9. Use questions, cues, and advanced organizers.

How do the nine work? We know that as humans we forget information quickly, so these strategies are ones that help us remember better, thus increasing the probability for deeper learning. When you go to the store, you make a list (note taking) so you remember what to buy. When you plan an event, you check with your friend (cooperative learning) to make sure that both of you remember to complete a particular task. You ask questions (cues and questions) for clarification, knowing you remember better when you connect it to what you know about and want to know. To plan or perform better, you might identify similarities or differences or predict with a hypothesis to try to know something more deeply. These nine are portable, practical, and powerful strategies that you use naturally when you think you might forget something or when you attempt to more deeply understand new information.

Since we can rely on most teachers using Hunter's daily routine, we blended the teaching routine with the learning strategies. We kept each of Hunter's steps (pedagogical automaticity) to cue the teacher to have students use one or more of the nine strategies at that specific point in each lesson. For example, if Hunter recommends that a teacher set an objective at the start of a lesson, and setting objectives and providing feedback is one of the nine strategies, then the teacher can explicitly plan to teach students how to set objectives for themselves and find productive ways to seek feedback.

By carrying over the successful familiar steps and updating some language from the *Mastery Teaching* model, the new schema became a teaching schema for *Master Learners*. It provided a way for a teacher to plan what she will do during a lesson and, importantly, for what she will explicitly teach and cue students to do so they can learn, remember, and apply the new information. GANAG refers to the steps below with shorthand abbreviations:

- **G**: Set the learning objective or **goal**. Students interact with objectives/goals unpacked from the standards.
- **A**: **Access** prior student knowledge. Students view visuals and cues, which encourages them to fire their neurons and share their background knowledge.
- **N**: Acquire **new information**. Students acquire the declarative or procedural knowledge about the objectives/goals.
- **A**: **Apply**. Students use thinking skills to learn declarative knowledge or practice procedural knowledge.

- **G**: **Goal review**. Students self-score to gauge their own progress on the standards (objectives/goals).

Assign homework, if necessary, to extend the lesson, and provide opportunities for feedback *at every step in the process* (self, peer, and expert).

GANAG and the Nine Strategies

GANAG lesson planning and delivery guides teachers through a five-step process to plan lessons that deliberately teach and provide time for students to use the nine strategies daily. As an example, teachers might consider embedding the nine strategies in the following way:

G: Goal/Objective
    Set objectives and provide feedback.
    Recognize effort and provide recognition.

A: Access Prior Knowledge
    Use nonlinguistic representations.
    Use cooperative learning.
    Use questions, cues, and advanced organizers.

N: New Information
    Take notes.
    Use cooperative learning.
    Use nonlinguistic representations.
    Use questions, cues, and advanced organizers.
    Practice.

A: Apply
    Practice.
    Identify similarities and differences.
    Generate and test hypotheses.
    Ask and answer analytical questions.

G: Goal Review
    Revisit objectives by intentionally scoring progress.
    Revisit effort.

GANAG in Detail

When students use the nine strategies daily to learn the content, they engage and reengage multiple times with the content and skills. Let's take a look at the lesson planning and delivery schema in detail.

Set the Goal/Objective: Write and Score

Many of today's teachers expect to teach to standards found in national, state, or subject-specific documents. The standards, as a rule, will be too broad for a daily lesson, so teachers unpack them, as we described in Chapter 2. We call those objectives or learning intentions the Gs of GANAG. For example, if the lesson addresses the science benchmark to "understand the complete mole concept and ways in which it can be used," then the Gs, or the specific content objectives, might include (1) know about actual mass versus relative mass, (2) know the relationship between the mole and the volume of a mole of molecules, and (3) know the relevance of molar volume and Avogadro's hypothesis. Although the teacher would likely teach to the standard for a number of days, those content objectives are the specific content for each day.

In an elementary classroom, the standard might be to "understand how different community members take responsibility for the common good," and the GANAG daily objectives could be to (1) know about individuals and what they do in a community, such as the mayor or director of parks and recreation, (2) know why some community members volunteer instead of work, and (3) know how groups within a community support causes, such as wildlife. Each day, the specific objectives could include studying leaders (e.g., the governor) and service workers (e.g., postal workers, firefighters, or librarians) and how they contribute to the common good. Many teachers write the objectives in "I can" or "I know" statements so they are more understandable for primary students.

Students use two of the nine strategies (setting objectives and providing feedback; reinforcing effort and providing recognition):

1. Students read the goal, repeat or discuss it, and write it.
2. Students score themselves on both their pre-understanding of the goal and how much effort they intend to expend during the lesson to learn the goal (we usually introduce effort scoring at about grade 2).

The teacher presents the goal to the students on a board or an electronic whiteboard and teaches the students to interact with the goal by self-assessing (see Figures 3.1 and 3.2). In a primary classroom, the teacher and students would say the goal aloud and then use hand signals, such as thumbs up, thumbs down, or thumbs to the side to indicate how well they know or can do the goal. In most other classrooms, the students would write the goal in a notebook, on a goal sheet, or online. Once written, the student would self-assess.

When a student writes down the goal, he pre-assesses how much he already knows about it and how much effort he anticipates applying to learning about it. Students use a simple scale, such as 1-2-3-4, to score themselves.

FIGURE 3.1

Elementary Goal Sheet

Name _____ Date _____

	Before	**Today I am learning about . . .**	**After**
Math	1 2 3 4		1 2 3 4
Reading	1 2 3 4		1 2 3 4
Writing	1 2 3 4		1 2 3 4
Science	1 2 3 4		1 2 3 4
Social Studies	1 2 3 4		1 2 3 4

1 = I am not too sure; **2** = I know a little or I need practice; **3** = I know all about it;
4 = I can teach a friend

Adapted by Susan Hensley, Rogers School District, Arkansas.

Consider how the beginning of a lesson changes for students. Instead of listening to the teacher discuss the goal and its importance, students are immediately engaged by writing down the goal and scoring their own understanding of it. The process becomes their habit; students learn to always take the first few minutes to focus on the learning objective. It is common to hear students come to class now asking, "What is the learning goal for today?"

This class-by-class routine prepares all students to know the lesson goal. By learning to self-score, students become aware of their own learning and learn how to gauge their own progress throughout each class and unit. Once students learn the routine, setting the goal should take two minutes at the beginning of every lesson. Later, at the end of the lesson (the second G of GANAG), we will revisit this self-assessment tool.

Access Prior Knowledge (APK): Everyone Participates

Most teachers learned to begin a lesson by asking a question designed to motivate or "hook" the students, yet teachers tell us that inevitably only two or three students ever respond. Hunter's intent for the "anticipatory set" was

FIGURE 3.2
Secondary Goal Sheet

Name _____   Unit/Chapter _____

Date	Goals and Objectives	Before Lesson	Pre-Class Effort	Post-Class Effort	After Lesson	Assignments or Assessments

1 = I need help or information; **2** = I need a refresher; **3** = I got it; **4** = I can pass the test now

Courtesy of St. John Vianney High School.

clear: the teacher should prepare a way to interest learners to anticipate the new learning.

Thirty years of learning research led us to update the phrase *anticipatory set* to *access prior knowledge,* which captures both the neurological concept of engaging background knowledge and the intention of preparing for new learning. In neurological terms, when neurons fire, then information connects and is more easily retrieved when you need it again. Donald Hebb's often quoted axiom about neurons that fire together, wire together, seems to apply here.

Let's see what it feels like to fire neurons. Consider what happens when we ask you to list all the words you associate with the word *cow.* Immediately, your neurons fire, and you might write *milk, pastures, barn, hay,* and *moo.* Now what happens if we ask you to list all the words you associate with the word *cambur?* Did you see pictures, think of smells, or hear anything, as you did with the prompt *cow?* Or did you draw a blank and then begin to try to figure out what the word might mean to you? (If you speak Spanish, *cambur* easily conjures the smells, colors, and experiences one knows about a lush tropical fruit: the banana.)

The beginning of the lesson should fire students' neurons in anticipation of the new information about to be learned; it should feel more like *cow* than *cambur* (unless, of course, you're in a Spanish class).

Certainly it is appropriate to have students review notes from previous days, work a problem on the board, or read a quotation from a text to discuss in anticipation of the new information. The reason for an APK is so every student fires neurons. With the advantages of today's technology, a teacher can show an image or video clip, play music, or conduct a brief demonstration to focus students' attention; he then prompts students to talk with a peer to encourage every student to actively engage. To guide the brief discussion, the teacher provides the cue or question. On a practical note, many teachers A-GNAG lessons; that is, they engage the students in the APK activity before presenting the G, or goal for the lesson.

An APK is short and sharp. It should take less than three minutes and involve all students by using three high-yield strategies (nonlinguistic representation; questions, cues, and advanced organizers; cooperative learning):

1. View an image or video, observe an object or movement, or listen to an anecdote, music, or sound.
2. Respond to a cue or question.
3. Pair/share with a peer.

One of our favorite APK stories comes from a secondary English classroom where the teacher, Dan Sullivan, was teaching students how to set a claim for an argument. To engage the students with the new content, he showed a slide of Jackson Pollock's 1952 painting *Number 11*, or *Blue Poles*. Giving his students a moment to see the splashes of paint characteristic of the artist, Dan said, "Tell your table partner whether or not the National Museum should have paid $1.3 million for this painting." Students responded enthusiastically with comments such as, "I could paint that for 1 million," or, "Splashed paint is not worth a million," or, "I believe Pollock's work is worth more than that!" The brief APK gave Mr. Sullivan the opportunity to say that most people can make impulsive claims, but he would teach them how to write claims that could be supported with evidence and information. Mr. Sullivan said that when he uses visuals and pair/shares, it is more likely that all of the students find a way to become engaged.

Most teachers tell us that once they get the hang of it, APKs are fun to plan and do in class. Here are a few examples:

1. Trista Spongberg taught the following Arkansas history standard to her kindergarten students: "Recognize state and national symbols that represent the local culture, heritage, and natural wonders." She displayed an image of the Coca-Cola logo on the electronic board and asked students to turn and talk with their "peanut butter and jelly" partners (pair and share). The students knew the symbol of the drink even though most of her young students could not yet read the text. She showed an image of the drink side by side with the logo. That was the transition to the new information, where they would learn about state and national symbols so they could learn to recognize them and know their importance.

2. Jacqueline Curlis taught her 3rd graders the math standard "Multiplication uses patterns to increase groups of equal parts." The unpacked objective read, "I can use small groups to make bigger groups." Ms. Curlis noticed that the students struggled with the concept of groups, so she used her APK to help the students access their knowledge to approach the new information. Since her class participated in the school basketball teams, she showed a picture of the different intramural groups wearing their different-colored jerseys. She asked her students to pair/share to describe how the class groups relate to the whole school group. Since the students could describe that, Ms. Curlis was able to teach about the math goal sure that all students understood the concept from a real-life example.

3. Fourth grade teacher Ms. Jones began a lesson by showing three famous images on a Google slide: Buzz Aldrin saluting the American flag on the moon (July 20, 1969), Marines raising the American flag at Iwo Jima (February 23, 1945), and firefighters hoisting the American flag at Ground Zero (September

11, 2001). Ms. Jones prompted her students, "What do these photographs have in common?" From that brief APK, she was able to teach the students about the standard related to procedures and etiquette for citizenship and flags.

4. In a grade 7 math class, Rupinder Grewal began the class about proper and improper fractions by showing a slide with the flags of Italy, Indonesia, Taiwan, Austria, Germany, and Spain. The cue was to write a fraction that represents what part of each flag is red. Once the students wrote a fraction for each of the flags, they shared with a partner to see if they agreed. During the APK, Ms. Grewal circulated to get a sense of how individual students understood fractions before she began to teach the lesson.

5. Secondary physical education teacher Eddie Bobell taught a class where they incorporated the GANAG framework into every lesson. On an introductory day when the students learned weightlifting techniques, they provided an APK activity where the students stacked golf balls for a couple of minutes before the instruction. In pairs, the students took turns encouraging each other and giving pointers. Then, they switched. Mr. Bobell used this brief APK to explain that it is easy to get frustrated when lifting weights but helpful to have someone encourage you and help. When the students went into the weight room, they were paired and prepared to do the same for each other.

Once more let's consider the level of engagement for all students in the class. When the teacher prepares a nonlinguistic representation (visual, movement, sound, object), then all students view it and can become involved in the conversation. By providing a cue and the direction to talk to a partner, every student engages as a way to anticipate the new information in the next part of the lesson.

The APK is not intended to be a review of the work from previous days or years. It is also not intended to "assess" prior knowledge. For teachers who want to review, they refer to GARNAG—that is, the short review that happens after the APK and before the new information.

Now that the APK has fired productive neurons, students are ready to acquire the new information.

Acquire New Information: Content and Skills

In this part of each lesson, teachers prepare to deliver the new information that students need to acquire. They plan for students to learn the new content through lectures, demonstrations, video, or readings, for example. One characteristic of GANAG is knowing whether you are teaching the students procedural or declarative knowledge. As stated by the goal for the lesson, the students will either learn the steps in a process (procedural knowledge), or they will learn information about a topic (declarative knowledge). As described in Chapter 2, we normally do not dissociate declarative and procedural knowledge in our day-to-day life, but when learning, we can. In either case, the students should take notes because it helps them retain the knowledge and also helps them process and ask more questions along the way. It may surprise some teachers to see our recommendation that the teacher explicitly teach note taking to pace the new information, even in the younger grades.

There are various methods for taking notes, such as an outline, Cornell, charting, and informal. Teachers can choose which one they prefer to use to teach the content. Because the GANAG schema was designed to engage and reengage students to use the nine strategies, we suggest that the teacher plan to teach content and skills but then provide intermittent stops with planned cues to allow students multiple opportunities to pause to process the new information. In this way, whether learning procedural or declarative knowledge, both types of information require the learner to stop briefly to practice (procedural) or process (declarative) the new information. Principal Dominick Radogna noted that his teachers refer to the new information part of the lesson as both the delivery of new content and the guided practice of a lesson. That helps remind teachers to teach and provide opportunities for students to process the information and seek feedback as they learn new information.

Four of the nine strategies can be incorporated into learning new information and the note-taking process:

1. Take notes.
2. Generate questions or answer questions.
3. Seek clarifying feedback from peers.
4. Add nonlinguistic sketches or images, such as a map or timeline, to notes.

Note taking with the opportunity to stop to process will help engage every student. The pauses also give students the chance to reengage, especially if they are checking in with a partner. In this way, students tend to be more active during the delivery of the new content in the lesson, whether it is a short 10-minute mini-lesson or 25 minutes long.

Some teachers like to teach students to use an interactive notebook with a teacher side and student side. It provides pacing in a lesson by cueing the teacher to stop periodically for the students to interact with the content on their side of the notebook. The teacher teaches for a few minutes while students take notes on the teacher side, then she pauses for students to ask or answer questions, add sketches, or summarize on the student side. The pauses give students opportunities to frequently, yet briefly, interact with peers for clarifying feedback. Similarly, "sketchnoting" is the process of taking both verbal and visual notes. When a student takes detailed notes about a topic, adding a visual can help them see the content, too. In today's information age, students are familiar with using icons and images, so it is natural for them to add sketches to notes. The Cornell note format gives students guidance on how to organize notes with the strategies above according to the teacher's pacing.

Let's consider a lesson that teaches procedural knowledge. When learning procedural information, such as solving equations, playing an instrument, using a reading strategy, or adding images to digital documents, the teacher demonstrates the new information in steps so that the students can take notes before they try the steps. Then they might practice and receive some correction. For example, when elementary school technology specialist George Santos introduces how to use a spreadsheet, he teaches step by step, pausing for students to write down the directions click by click; then they try a few times before moving ahead. Usually there are not a lot of notes for procedural knowledge, but the steps are useful to have written, as it takes practice to make them automatic.

When a lesson goal is highly declarative, the teacher prepares a lecture, shows video, or provides readings. The elementary mini-lesson may be 10 minutes, but a secondary history or biology lesson may require 20–25 minutes of new information. Using any of the note-taking suggestions above and pausing to process knowledge so students receive feedback from the teacher, peers, or self is critical throughout a lesson because it helps students engage and reengage with the content.

Apply Knowledge: Thinking and Practice

The second A of GANAG stands for *application*, when students have the opportunity to apply the new information independently, whether it is procedural or declarative knowledge.

When planning for students to apply declarative knowledge, thinking skills (e.g., comparing, analyzing for errors, making decisions) can help the learner organize facts to first retain the information longer and then generate new ideas. Various frameworks for thinking skills are available both in print and online. It is important to note that teachers should teach the thinking skill as part of the new information, and they should direct students to use it for the application. Among the nine high-yield strategies are three categories (identifying similarities and differences, generating and testing hypotheses, and questioning) that further expand to a dozen robust thinking skills. In Chapter 4 we will discuss the thinking skills in more detail.

As for procedural knowledge, research shows it takes about 24 practices (Marzano, Pickering, & Pollock, 2001) for someone to learn a new procedure to a level of competency. Although 24 sounds like an unreasonable number, if you think about it in terms of separate days of schooling, in reality it's manageable. Just remember the days when you first learned how to do something, like edit a video clip or use grading software. Although it might have seemed to take forever, after about seven tries, you could do it without referring to the steps. It took a few more practices for you to shape the skill so you could use it strategically.

GANAG specifies that when new information is declarative knowledge, the students should follow two steps:

1. Learn the new content.
2. Apply a thinking skill from the nine strategies, like comparing (identifying similarities and differences), argument (analytical questions), and experimental inquiry (generating and testing hypotheses).

If the lesson goal is procedural knowledge, the students should

1. Learn the steps in the new content with guided practice.
2. Practice the steps (practice) to the point of automaticity in new situations and seek constructive feedback from self, peers, and the teacher.

The last part of the application section of GANAG might include summarizing the learning in a student's own words in his notebook. Because content can vary, GANAG has to be flexible. Many teachers discuss varying the amount of new information or application depending on the lesson: GANaG or GAnAG. When teaching procedural knowledge, most teachers say that they GAnanananaG lessons.

Goal Review: Student Self-Assessment

The last G of GANAG stands for goal review. It is the time for learners to again score their understanding of the lesson objective and compare their score before the lesson. Students can also gain insight into how effort can affect learning if they also rated how much effort they intended to expend. Students once more engage in using two high-yield strategies (setting objectives and providing feedback; reinforcing effort and providing recognition).

For a couple of minutes, the teacher walks around the classroom scanning notebooks or score sheets to see how students report on their own understandings or abilities to perform the skills. These scores provide both the students and the teacher feedback about the lesson and the learning. Teachers can potentially use this form of formative or self-assessment to help inform changes to subsequent instruction for one or more students.

It takes a couple of weeks for students to realize the power of the goal review. At first, it is just what they do at the end of the lesson, but as they learn to track their own progress, they see how much they learn and how important it is to the teacher to write down their scores. In time, the habit of self-scoring empowers students to seek feedback on their own and ask for further instruction.

Extending the Lesson with Homework

Homework can extend the school day, if necessary. Teachers assign homework to broaden the scope of declarative or procedural knowledge for the learner. Completing relevant readings, taking notes, or creating a graphic organizer on the day's lesson can all be useful in accomplishing this extension of knowledge. The homework assignment can then be used the next day in school to add new information. Homework is also a useful tactic when students need unsupervised practice for the procedural knowledge they learn.

Using today's technology, many teachers have successfully flipped their lessons or added assignments that can be turned in electronically. This helps increase feedback to students in a timely and productive way.

Feedback, Feedback, Feedback

Although not numbered in the core list of steps, the opportunities for various forms of feedback are critical. The reality is, as soon as you set the goal or the objective for the class, the feedback process can begin. Feedback should be directly related to the goals and objectives for the day in order for the student to make improvements. Teachers who understand the importance of feedback to the learner can vary the types of feedback (verbal and nonverbal or written), the voices of feedback (self-reflection, peer, and teacher), and the opportunities for or timeliness of feedback comments. The feedback steps, then, occur throughout each lesson.

Each of the steps in GANAG provides an opportunity for students to seek and receive feedback in every class. The goal setting and scoring is a way to operationalize self-feedback; the cooperative pair/sharing throughout the APK, new information, and application are chances for peer feedback; and the actively engaged students in the note taking, practicing, and thinking skills gives teachers opportunities to walk around the class providing formative feedback to individual students each day.

GANAG and Technology

One of the best parts of teaching in the 21st century is access to devices and the internet. With so many resources available, the teacher can plan to use them for organization and efficiency as well as to give students the opportunity to learn how to access useful information. Whether it is the visual for the APK or the video for new information, GANAG recommends that students be able to use devices to access the information about the content or procedural knowledge, as well as produce their own original work.

For many teachers and students, remote learning has become a reality. When teaching in remote learning environments, teachers say they are glad to have GANAG to help engage students who may be in various different places, including at home. Many teachers find the Gs of GANAG have strengthened their remote learning classes because the lesson begins and ends with students having a specific task to do.

Getting the Lesson Plan on the Page

At first glance, GANAG seems to be a rigid set of steps, but as teachers plan, they realize that yes, because GANAG is about student learning, every lesson should engage students with the G-A and then close with the last G. But, many teachers will AGNAG their lessons, using the APK as a way to draw students to the goal. Finally, if one does want to teach an inquiry lesson, it might look like this sequence: APK, application, goal, new information, and goal review (AAGNG).

As we discussed in Chapter 2, teachers can begin unit planning with the one-pager. At that point, the teacher can begin to plan the day-to-day lessons, including where to place assessment tasks.

Planning is personal, so teachers use different ways to organize their lessons. Figure 3.3 shows a weekly planner some teachers use to link their resources. Figure 3.4 shows an elementary planner.

Changing Pedagogical Automaticity

Brenda Turner, assistant principal at Nicolet High School in Wisconsin, observed that embracing the Big Four works because it provides a framework that incorporates high-yield instructional strategies with tangible techniques for learning. But pedagogical automaticity, particularly after several years of teaching, can be challenging to change. So she suggests each teacher completes a personal needs assessment as a starting point and accordingly adjusts

FIGURE 3.3
Weekly Template

	Monday	Tuesday	Wednesday	Thursday	Friday
Standards:					
G	Goal/Objective:	Goal/Objective:	Goal/Objective:	Goal/Objective:	Goal/Objective:
A	Visual: Cue:	Visual: Cue:	Visual: Cue:	Visual: Cue:	Visual: Cue:
N	PPT:	PPT:	PPT:	PPT:	
A					
G	Goal Sheets:	Goal Sheets:	Goal Sheets:	Goal Sheets:	Goal Sheets:

FIGURE 3.4

Elementary Planner for GANAG

Monday	Tuesday	Wednesday
8:40–9:00 Arrival	8:40–9:00 Arrival	8:40–9:00 Arrival
9:00–9:30 Morning Meeting G: A: N: A: G:	**9:00–9:30 Morning Meeting** G: A: N: A: G:	**9:00–9:30 Morning Meeting** G: A: N: A: G:
9:30–10:30 Math Lesson # ~ Homelink	**9:30–10:30 Math** Lesson # ~ Homelink	**9:30–10:30 Math** Lesson # ~ Homelink
10:30–11:00 Science/Social Studies G: A: N: A: G:	**10:30–11:00 Science/Social Studies** G: A: N: A: G:	**10:30–11:00 Science/Social Studies** G: A: N: A: G:
11:05–11:35 Lunch	**11:05–11:35 Lunch**	**11:05–11:35 Lunch**
11:35–12:00 Word Study Lesson/page #	**11:35–12:00 Word Study** Lesson/page #	**11:35–12:00 Word Study** Lesson/page #
12:00–12:25 Playtime	12:00–12:25 Playtime	12:00–12:25 Playtime
12:30–1:10 Specials	12:30–1:10 Specials	12:30–1:10 Specials
1:15–3:15 Language Arts **1:15–2:00 Guided Reading** **2:00–2:30 Conferences**	**1:15 –3:15 Language Arts** **1:15–2:00 Guided Reading** **2:00–2:30 Conferences**	**1:15–3:15 Language Arts** **1:15–2:00 Guided Reading** **2:00–2:30 Conferences**
2:15–2:25 Book Buddies **2:25–2:30 Literature Share** **2:30–3:15 Writing Workshop** G: A: N: A: G:	**2:00–2:15 Independent Read** **2:15–2:25 Book Buddies** **2:25–2:30 Literature Share** **2:30–3:15 Writing Workshop** G: A: N: A: G:	**2:15–2:25 Book Buddies** **2:25–2:30 Literature Share** **2:30–3:15 Writing Workshop** G: A: N: A: G:

Thursday	Friday	Notes
8:40–9:00 Arrival	8:40–9:00 Arrival	
9:00–9:30 Morning Meeting Literacy G: A: N: A: G:	**9:00–9:30 Morning Meeting Literacy** G: A: N: A: G:	
9:30–10:30 Math Lesson # Homelink	**9:30–10:30 Math** Lesson # Homelink	
10:30–11:00 Science/Social Studies G: A: N: A: G:	**10:30–11:00 Science/Social Studies** G: A: N: A: G:	
11:05–11:35 Lunch	**11:05–11:35 Lunch**	**Meetings**
11:35–12:00 Word Study Lesson/page #	**11:35–12:00 Word Study** Lesson/page #	
12:00–12:25 Playtime	12:00–12:25 Playtime	**Newsletter Info**
12:30–1:10 Specials	12:30–1:10 Specials	
1:15–3:15 Language Arts **1:15–2:00 Literacy** G: A: N: A: G: **2:00–2:15 Conferences** **2:00–2:15 Independent Read** **2:15–2:25 Book Buddies** **2:25–2:30 Literature Share** **2:30–3:15 Writing Workshop** G: A: N: A: G:	**1:15–3:15 Language Arts** **1:15–2:00 Guided Reading** **2:00–2:15 Independent Read** **2:15–2:25 Book Buddies** **2:25–2:30 Literature Share** **2:30–3:15 Writing Workshop** G: A: N: A: G:	

Adapted from Michelle Crisafulli, Reynolds Elementary School, Baldwinsville, New York.

lesson planning and delivery practices little by little—as Gary Nunnally, Belinda Parini, and Jennifer Collins have done—to improve student learning for all.

Rate the following statements: 1 = Never … 4 = Always.

- I utilize the GANAG lesson design or another research-based lesson design when planning.
- I have clear learning targets for lessons that are clearly communicated with the students.
- My students assess themselves on the learning targets before and after each lesson.
- I activate prior knowledge before beginning a lesson.
- I know and embed many high-yield instructional strategies into my lessons on a regular basis.
- I frequently collect feedback on student learning to inform my instruction.
- I create multiple opportunities for students to process information.
- I recognize the difference between declarative and procedural knowledge and use this information to drive instructional decisions.
- I only give homework for practice as an extension of the school day.
- I provide timely, meaningful feedback on all homework.

Summary

Teachers know the value of students staying active during a class period. The GANAG schema contributes to both teacher preparation for materials and delivery of content, as well as the cue to engage and reengage students frequently throughout a class period. The routine, like any habit, takes some time to shape during the first few weeks, but soon enough it becomes the new pedagogy for many teachers. Principal Tracey Sorrentino commented that the value of GANAG is how it creates student learning habits. When students go to every class—math, English, visual arts, PE, history, science, and so forth—they begin to notice that it changes how they learn. The routine starts with their goal setting, which begins the process for them to seek feedback. With daily practice in every class, teachers say that using GANAG allows them more opportunities to catch students learning as well as differentiate or catch in real time each day.

The next two chapters move the discussion from instruction to assessing student performance with the standards. It is useful to divide assessment into two Chapter 4 takes a look at designing assessment tasks for the classroom, including critical and creative thinking skills. Chapter 5 discusses the particulars about scoring to standards as a way to improve feedback to students so they perform better.

Teacher Voice
Jennifer Collins, *Math Teacher in Tennessee*

My experience with lesson planning changed dramatically from university to when I stepped into a 7th and 8th grade math classroom in a pre-K through 12 school. After having the flexibility in college to pick standards and spend a lot of time creating activities for the ones I liked the best, I soon realized that my teaching job involved interpreting *all* of the state standards to determine how the students would demonstrate mastery of those expectations. I had prepared for the job by reviewing the standards the state identified for 7th and 8th grade math. The standards were not fun, and I lacked a firm understanding of many of the expectations. I also lacked the many hours needed to create the perfect lesson plan for each day. As enthusiasm gave way to panic, I spoke with other teachers about my concerns. They advised, "Just follow the book and teach whatever it tells you." This concept seemed simple enough. After all, this is the method I suspect that most of my own teachers had used.

I just kept turning the page, and the book told me what to teach each day.

As the spring semester started, my assistant principal brought me an end-of-year assessment prep book that he had purchased for both grade levels. Each lesson in the book was closely tied to the state's standards, and I quickly realized that the textbook I had depended so heavily on was not well aligned. I knew at that point I was in trouble and there was no way that I could teach everything I needed to before the end-of-year achievement test.

That same semester, a few teachers in my school district began to use a lesson planning schema they learned in a professional development session. I was drowning and excited to receive any help that was available. I joined them and began to learn the basics of how to GANAG a lesson. That was when my pedagogy began to change and my students started to perform to the expectations.

Setting the Goal

GANAG teaches that the goal is the most important aspect of a lesson. In the past, I would determine a topic for my lessons. The topics would be generic. Rather than deconstructing state standards and expectations, I would use vague descriptions such as two-step equations. While working with GANAG, I quickly realized the importance of a goal. Understanding the expectations and settings the goal(s) for each math standard was the hardest part of lesson planning for me. Our state standards were not in teacher- or student-friendly language, but I knew that if my students were going to succeed, I would have to decode each standard and write them in objective language.

I began by setting small attainable goals that were scaffolded toward student mastery for each of the broad standards created by the state. This did not come easy, and it took several months to really understand my standards and master the art of goal setting.

The next challenge was to have my students interact with the goal. I began having my students track the goals in their notebooks. They would write the goal. Next, we would read the goal. Finally, to clarify understanding and set the expectations, we would discuss the goal and they could self-score. My students not only knew what to expect for the day, but their math vocabulary began to expand. They began using the word *coefficient* rather than "that number in front of *x*." They began to be more successful with word problems because they were interacting with the vocabulary in their daily goals. In turn, the word problems and vocabulary were tied to an activity that related back to the daily goals.

Accessing Prior Knowledge

Accessing prior knowledge (APK) serves the purpose of preparing the students for the learning. It engages the thinking process and sparks their curiosity.

Finding the perfect APK can oftentimes be difficult. It can also become a task that will alter the way you look at everyday activities. You begin to find ideas for APKs everywhere. My husband is also a teacher who uses GANAG. There have been many conversations that have ended with "That would make a great APK." We recently purchased a 65-inch television and could not fit it into our car to take it home. After begging the manager to go against policy and let us pick it up in the morning, my husband and I began to panic about borrowing a vehicle that would be large enough to haul our new purchase. I called my dad and asked to borrow his much larger vehicle, but we were still worried the television would not fit. We did not know the width of the television, only that the diagonal measurement was 65 inches. When I measured the width of my dad's vehicle, it was exactly 65 inches. My husband and I, again, began to panic because the only length of the television that we knew was the diagonal, and it was exactly 65 inches. Suddenly my math brain kicked in and I remembered the Pythagorean theorem. The diagonal is the hypotenuse, and the hypotenuse is always the longest length; therefore, the width of the TV would be less than 65 inches and fit just fine. I looked at my husband with a huge smile on my face and said, "This is going to make the greatest APK ever!"

New Information

Each lesson a teacher presents requires new information. Sometimes it is procedural knowledge that students need in order to solve an expression. Other times it is declarative knowledge that they will need to solve real-world math tasks. Whichever the case, when delivering new information, I learned to anticipate my students' needs. It is important to me to be prepared to provide them as much support on the new material as possible.

To ensure my students were not lost during this process, I continually relied on a student-driven feedback loop. I needed to know the new information was being internalized and stored for future application. I used many strategies to determine if my students understood the information. My favorite formative assessment was student use of personal whiteboards. I would deliver new information for five minutes, allowing my students time to try what I modeled and demonstrate their understanding. Their answers would tell me if I needed to continue instruction, back up, or provide more support. I would also use this feedback to determine which students needed additional help once we moved on to the application part of the lesson. Some students needed a small group setting when learning new concepts. I would use the feedback during the new information portion to determine who needed to be grouped for further instruction as my other students continued on independently.

Apply the New Information

When planning for the application of the new information, I always referred back to the lesson's goal. The application piece must ensure that students are demonstrating the action part of the daily goal. For example, if the goal was "I can write equations in slope-intercept form when they are given in standard form," I would give my students a set of equations that were written in standard form and require them to rewrite the equations in slope-intercept form. I did not want to give them a set of equations in slope-intercept form and then require them to graph the equations. Graphing, while an important algebraic application, was not a part of the goal that was set forward for the day and therefore should not be the focus of the application process.

On some days, we used the thinking skills as a way to get a deeper understanding of the math concepts. Often that meant reviewing the steps to the thinking skills before we start to apply them in this part of the lesson. A lot of math instruction needs to be procedural, so every time I teach a thinking skill it always amazes me how productive it turns out for students deeply learning the concepts.

Goal Review

At the end of each lesson, it is important for my students and me to reflect on the day's learning. There have been many times when I thought a lesson was successful, but when I completed my goal review, I found out it was not as successful as I expected. I went back and thought about what the goal asked my students to demonstrate for the day. If I wanted to ensure that my students comprehended procedural knowledge, I would give my students a procedural problem to solve before they gave themselves scores on their goal sheets. If my goal for the day required declarative knowledge, I would have given my students a word problem or ask them to write a note to explain what they learned to another student. Then, they would rescore on their goal sheets. When students left my classroom, their scores gave me a glance into how they would do the next day.

Looking Ahead

When I began teaching, I had no idea how to begin planning for everyday lessons. I had only experienced planning for evaluation purposes—that is, to evaluate me as a teacher. Applying the GANAG lesson plan schema allowed me to focus on making sure students really understood and were able to do the math throughout various parts of a daily lesson. I began to learn how to write this information in shorthand while internalizing the planning routine. As I transition into a new position as a curriculum coach, I use the GANAG format with my teachers not only to increase our ability to communicate but also to help them improve their students' learning.

4

Assessment Tasks

A friend of ours who is a high school principal says that he hears from both parents and teachers that too much class time is taken up by testing. One perception is that state testing takes time away from instruction, and thus teachers say they are reluctant to add more classroom tests for the same reason. "I understand that folks don't like the state testing because it seems that it doesn't really help the students, and a reality in many states is that results are not received in a timely manner or in a format that easily impacts instruction. But, classroom testing—research is pretty clear that it is mostly beneficial. How can we help teachers find a way to include more testing and show positive benefits?"

Let's consider positive aspects of classroom assessment. In most subjects, after a couple of weeks of instruction students take a test to show what they understand and remember how to do. Who benefits? Students do, because it confirms their knowledge and performance. Teachers benefit because they can reteach or move ahead to the next topics knowing how well students mastered the content and skills. Parents or caregivers benefit, as it provides a snapshot of their child's work at school. In *Make It Stick: The Science of Successful Learning*, Brown, Roediger, and McDaniel (2014) note that "In virtually all areas of learning, you build better mastery when you use testing as a tool to identify and bring up your areas of weakness" (p. 5). Assessment has been useful for years because it works to confirm or document performance levels, but as these researchers wrote, new research shows the importance of testing as a tool to learn material more deeply and identify the areas upon which to improve.

To improve student testing results, it is common to see recommendations, such as teaching test-taking skills or varying the assessments themselves. There is much written about types of assessment, such as forced-choice versus constructed-response, including what appears to be a bias that labels projects as authentic assessment tasks. In many cases, teachers spend time developing different tests, but while the assessment tools improve, the student learning gains do not seem in proportion with the work. There is no doubt it is important to improve tests; however, in this chapter, we limit our recommendations to address a few assessment techniques shown to increase learning and complement the classroom chapter or unit tests.

Chapter 1 explained assessment in the Big Four as a way to maximize feedback and require critical and creative thinking. Teachers should use formative assessment to provide timely feedback and redesign some assessments using critical and creative thinking skills. All assessments should directly tie back to the curriculum standards, providing the scaffolds and modifications for students to show their best work.

In the beginning of this chapter, we address two types of assessment that require very little class time and have significantly increased achievement for all students. Because they are two types of formative assessment, teachers can take the opportunity to provide reteaching or differentiation as the students learn the material. The assessments include (1) a student self-assessment technique adapted to the Gs of GANAG and (2) standards checks, or frequent quizzes to check understanding.

In the second part of this chapter, we discuss critical and creative thinking skills. In Chapter 3, we introduced the idea of teaching students to use thinking skills so they could deepen their understanding of conceptual knowledge. At that time, we noted that this chapter would provide a more detailed discussion about thinking skills. Here we address teachers' questions about how to teach students to learn more deeply so they can construct original responses on essays and answer open-ended questions with fluency.

Formative and Summative Assessment

Any discussion about classroom assessment should probably start with definitions. Formative assessment occurs as students are *forming* their learning, and summative assessment is the *sum* of learning a topic, referring to the time frame. The terms can be confusing because summative tasks tend to clearly describe the unit tests or term tests, but the nature of what constitutes formative assessment seems ambiguous. Are all tasks that provide feedback formative? Do students always need to receive feedback immediately if the task is intended as formative? Do teachers have to design formative assessments and give them as quizzes?

Typically, summative tests happen at the end of a course (usually in secondary schools), mid-semester, and at the end of each unit, often determined by either the text or the curriculum pacing guides. Because of the timing of the tasks, they are often designed to be scored or marked quickly; they tend to have more short answer or forced choice, except in areas such as English, where there is often an essay or writing component. These assessments provide evidence or grades that teachers use to report student progress and often are averaged for a final mark for a course. The summative assessment does not generally provide multiple opportunities for retakes since the intention is the sum or completion of the work. Because there are few opportunities to relearn the materials, the practice of summative testing generally will not result in gains in student achievement. Formative assessment does.

Formative assessment is much more flexible and provides opportunities for continued instruction and learning after the assessment. Formative assessment, therefore, should be brief, frequent, and timely. If "forming" learning equates to being during instructional times, then formative assessment occurs while students are in the middle of learning about a topic or a skill. Formative assessment can occur after a day or two of instruction, knowing the topic will continue for another lesson or more. The data provide the teacher ample options for differentiation and reteaching as needed. Formative assessment might take the form of a quiz that can be marked by the students, because the clear intention is that they are getting an opportunity to check in on what they remember and how well they can perform. Other types of formative assessment include teacher observation or self-scoring; both offer timely feedback and the opportunity to relearn material. When teachers commit to increasing formative assessment opportunities in class, student engagement and achievement increase.

Student Self-Assessment

We usually think of assessment as a quiz or test, but in this section, we describe how teachers teach students to use the student self-assessment technique adapted to the beginning of the lesson when the teacher sets the objective (the high-yield strategy to set objectives and provide feedback). Students learn to score themselves on the lesson goals at the beginning and end of each lesson. Over time, students understand that (1) they will learn something every day in every class, (2) the self-assessment allows them to communicate to the teacher their understandings and performances tied to the learning goal, and (3) they can see how their daily self-scores relate to better quiz and test scores. While it may not seem exciting, the habit of self-scoring is motivating because it teaches students the importance of meeting smaller goals to reach larger goals. This type of formative assessment is productive and powerful because it teaches students to have a voice in their own learning.

In John Hattie's (2009) synthesis of meta-analyses, *Visible Learning*, he writes about self-reported grades, "Students have reasonably accurate understandings of their levels of achievement; the effect size is a very high 1.44" (p. 43). His interpretation of the data is that students come to school with background knowledge about how well they do in academic situations, adding that many do not consider themselves to have the necessary skills or knowledge base. Then, in a very salient manner, he adds the promising comment "But one of the most fascinating outcomes of meta-analyses is that there are measures that schools can implement that are more influential than this prior achievement effect" (p. 44). The self-scoring technique is one of the ways that students gain the confidence that they are learning and that every lesson contributes to the gains.

There are at least three ways that teachers can teach students to self-score: using goal sheets, in notebooks, and electronically. Here are some examples of each.

Goal Sheets

Primary students who are beginning to learn to write can develop good self-assessment habits. At the beginning of every class, the teacher shows the learning goal (unpacked standard) for the lesson on the electronic whiteboard (or on the whiteboard or easel). The teacher reads aloud the goal and the students repeat it. He may focus on the key academic vocabulary in the statement, underlining it so students are keenly aware of the new concept or skill. He might ask the students to show their scores (1-2-3-4) with their hands before writing and scoring. After setting a timer, the teacher tells students they have two minutes to write the goal and score themselves with a goal sheet like the example in Figure 3.1. Next to the statement, each student circles the number in the rubric that may read something like the following: 4, I can help a friend; 3, I can do this myself; 2, I need some help; 1, I need help.

The teacher walks around looking over the student work, nudging and confirming. Then, the class moves into the next part of the lesson. At the end of that lesson, the students have a similar opportunity to rescore themselves. The teacher may ask how many moved from a lower score to a higher one based on the lesson.

Since some students may need some modifications, teachers say they sometimes give the students the goal already written or partially written so they can glue it into their notebooks. Once in a while, students may receive an organizer to work on during the lesson, so the goal may already be written at the top of the page with the numbers on either side. Those strategies vary depending on the lessons and for any English language learners (ELLs) and students with special needs.

Many middle and high school teachers use the goal sheet as a unit divider. Using a goal sheet like the one in Figure 3.2, Tyler Jones teaches the students to self-score but adds a few more sophisticated steps. In addition to scoring content knowledge, the secondary students are asked to score themselves on how much effort they required (recognize effort and provide recognition). When they score themselves at the end, many realize that effort affects performance; the more effort you put in, the better you do. Also, the secondary teachers added the assignment/assessment column so students can add their scores back to the score sheet a few days later; it tells them when they think they understand or can do something at the end of the lesson and whether or not it is true a few days later. Students identify this technique as probably the most powerful for preparing for tests.

Notebook Headers

Teachers at Monhagen Middle School teach students to write the goal at the top of the notebook page where they will take notes about that topic. English teacher Kerrianne Miranda said that the students use a table of contents in their notebooks for the topic, but they prefer their goals on the page where they take notes. They add the knowledge and effort scores next to the goal. The teacher puts the goal on the whiteboard or electronic board and walks around the room, quietly taking attendance and glancing at their sheets. Once the students have the goal on their notes page, it is practical for the teacher or the student to return to the goal at various points during the new information part of the lesson in order to check in and gauge progress.

Before the class ends, a student reminds the teachers that they have a few minutes before the bell, so they self-score again. The bookends of every lesson give students a way to focus on the content of the lesson and also on their own academic behavior. Often a student proudly acknowledges gains and draws the teacher's attention to the scoring. Everyone always knows what they are learning about each day, and teachers tell us they notice that it increases engagement throughout the lesson.

Electronic Goal Sheets

Secondary teacher Vincent Barone uses goal sheets but has incorporated them into a digital platform. The students have electronic goal sheets on their class webpage, and when he puts the goal on the slide, they use a word processor to score themselves the same as they would if it were in the print notebook. Mr. Barone can see on his device as the students score themselves, but he also walks around the room as encouragement. With frequent quizzes, the students can see their own progress and where they may need reteaching. The digital platform allows some of the reteaching to be done through video or other electronic sources.

In some classes, such as physical education or drama, where the facility does not lend itself to easy use of notebooks or devices, teachers can say the goal aloud and have students share with a partner or physically move into a space to indicate scores by groupings. Teachers should show flexibility so that students know how important it is that they know the goal.

Students with special needs and ELLs may need more assistance during the goal setting part of the lesson, and a digital platform allows for personalization. Some teachers prepare the goal sheets with some of the text already written. In some resource classrooms, the teachers may read the goal aloud and have students use manipulatives to indicate their self-scores before they write them in notebooks or goal sheets.

Besides focusing the students' attention on the content of the lesson, scoring to the Gs of GANAG teach students that they are responsible for their own learning. They know very well to what extent they understand or can do the goal, so this gives them time to reflect, and it also makes their personal evaluation visible to the teacher on a daily basis. Generally, the only days when the students do not self-score are testing days.

Standards Checks and Frequent Quizzes

As referenced earlier, Brown, Roediger, and McDaniel researched how students study and made a case for frequent quizzes so that students learn material and retain it longer. The authors argue that most of the strategies that people use to try to learn and retain information, such as rereading, highlighting, underlining, or repeating it over and over, are among the least productive or, as they say, are a waste of time. In other words, many of the strategies that students use to study for tests don't work. They cite dozens of examples of research in schools and universities that led them to suggest that learners benefit from frequent quizzing. In addition to the quizzes, they recommend that some material be carried across multiple quizzes, known as interleaving, to interrupt the forgetting curve.

The authors suggest short standards checks as opportunities to test content with some interleaving criteria. In subjects like math, standards checks require students to remember some of the recurring procedures that they often forget, such as working with decimals or negative numbers or completing multistep problems. In subjects like science or history, standards checks could include questions from earlier units.

Standards checks are formative assessment tasks that look like and are administered as quizzes. A typical standards check in a math class is four questions related to a math standard; the students complete it in less than 10 minutes. Because the questions are leveled from least complex to most complex, students know that if they can accurately complete all four questions, then they get a score of 4. If they are unable to answer the third and fourth questions, then they are at a 2 level on that standard. In a science or social studies class, the standards checks can be multiple choice or short answer. In English classes, many of the standards checks are recurring because the skills have to be applied in many different types of texts. The readings in the standards checks would differ, but the questions can essentially address some of the standards that frequently appear in standardized tests.

The standards checks are designed to follow about two or three days of instruction so that students are given frequent opportunities to check their own understanding. These formative assessments are marked at the end of the 10 minutes, and the teacher can use the information to differentiate for further instruction *in that lesson* or be mindful of the scores to prepare for differentiation in the subsequent lesson. Since it is a quiz, students should work independently.

Rusty Bishop's Algebra 1 and 2 student scores increased from 38 percent passing to consistently showing passing rates at the 80 percent level after incorporating the standards checks. Special educator Tara Markle and specialist Rachel Koontz adapted formative assessment to make "quick checks," one or two questions for students to show their work and provide data for reteaching. The students like the quick checks, and they help them retain the information for the tests.

Science teacher McKinzie Sanders began to use quizzes instead of reviews for unit tests. It began when she played a scavenger hunt game with students one day before a test; she would ask a question and students had to find the answer to the question in their notes. Soon she realized that students wanted to answer first and then check themselves. Since it was like a game, they started to use the quizzes more frequently, which improved their scores and note taking. The students also added flashcards and pictographs to their studying.

Since many students love electronic quiz games, such as Kahoot, teachers can use them at either the beginning or end of classes. Rather than creating long, 30-item quizzes, the teacher should develop multiple short quizzes of only four or five questions, interleaving the content so that students have the opportunity to remember some of the information from previous days.

One of the findings that surprised the authors of *Make It Stick: The Science of Successful Learning* (Brown et al., 2014) is that teachers should announce quizzes and not try to use a surprise technique. More frequent, announced quizzes encourages students to take better notes in class, be prepared for the quizzes, and notice their improved scores on tests as a result.

Testing Thinking

The recommendation to assess students' critical and creative thinking is echoed through initiatives that date back as far as Horace Mann in the 1840s. After administering the first standardized test in Boston, the secretary of the Massachusetts State Board of Education stated, "What little students knew came from memorizing the textbook without having to think about the meaning of what they learned" (Rothstein, 1998, p. 17). One hundred years later, Bloom's taxonomy would echo the sentiment. Teachers are familiar with Norman Webb's Depth of Knowledge, which identifies four levels of assessment, with the two higher levels indicating higher-order thinking. Today, 21st century standards developed by the International Society for Technology in Education (ISTE) include *knowledge constructor* and *innovative designer*, defined as critical and creative thinkers.

In this section, we address how to assess thinking skills but explain that, in order to do so, it is important to *teach* critical and creative thinking. Also, to teach critical and creative thinking, the students need time to gather and organize significant amounts of knowledge. We begin with a story by Billy Donohue, a social studies teacher and football coach.

Tennis Balls and Hula Hoops

As part of our fall football program, we held a variety of camps in the off season for our athletes to install new schemes, test new ideas, and bring new coaches into the fold. I tried to recruit new coaches out of college because they had fresh ideas and enthusiasm. Every year, I would give them an opportunity to organize the individual position drills. By removing myself from the drills, I could evaluate the coaches. I noticed a trend—new coaches always had really innovative drills that always seemed to involve equipment like tennis balls and hula hoops. The drills were highly engaging, and the players seemed excited and clearly had fun, but there seemed to be little connection between drills and actual situations that the athletes would encounter during a game.

Following the practice, during debriefing, I would ask, "Why did you choose those particular drills?" The answers were always the same—they found great ideas online, and the players really liked doing them. I would then pull out the playbook and go through the basic fundamental skills required by position. For instance, wide receivers need to get in stances, get off the line, block, catch, and run routes. I would then ask them how their drills prepared the athletes for these expectations, and honestly, most of the time, they did not. My goal was not to embarrass or upset the coaches; rather, I wanted to use this as a teachable moment. We had a set of expectations outlined in the playbook, and using them to design drills was essential for preparing our students for the big test: Friday night.

"Now let me tell you about classroom assessment, and you will understand why I told you the football story," he said. Billy, now a school administrator, remembers when he was a teacher and his principal advised that he "vary the assessment" in his class. The directive implied that the teacher would give fewer "traditional" paper-and-pencil multiple-choice tests and essays. So Billy, like many other teachers, designed projects based on more performance and communication—skits, posters, commercials, physical models—that gave the sense of more authentic assessment. He continued:

> Always thinking of ways to make history more relevant to help students see the importance of the content, I decided to bring the French Revolution unit to life: we would put King Louis XVI on trial! I spent an inordinate amount of time assembling print and nonprint sources to establish the descriptions of all of the roles for the trial. I set aside two weeks for students to spend class time preparing for their respective roles. When the big day finally came, my students rose to the occasion. The trial went extremely well; the students had a fun and memorable experience. At the end of the unit, the students took the summative assessment, and most did poorly on the content related to the history of the revolution. What happened? The trial was a tremendously valuable experience—is this not what we wanted for our students? Hadn't the project assessment required critical and creative thinking?

Now I see that the experience was tennis balls and hula hoops. I thought they would think more deeply about the historical event if they engaged in a more creative task. Anyway, it didn't work. I'm coaching a teacher who is at the point of the French Revolution in her pacing guide, and I want to be able to show her how to teach students to think deeply, make meaning, and remember the important historical information. It would be great to design a project, but is there a way to make it a thinking task that helps students deepen their knowledge about the standards?

In a similar exchange, kindergarten (prep) teacher Sarah Fletcher told us she wasn't sure she was actually teaching and assessing student thinking as much as noticing when a few of her students seemed to share unusually creative ideas. Her lessons always involve lots of materials, such as those in a recycling unit or about different animal adaptations, that lend themselves to her posing lots of guiding questions, prompting many opportunities for clever responses. Looking back, she said there were just as many basic answers as creative ones. Sarah, like many other primary teachers, wanted a way to teach and assess thinking for all students. "We teach students steps to do a lot of things like graphing or writing, so it seems like there could be steps to teaching thinking," she said.

Both Billy and Sarah recognized how much effort they put into planning engaging projects, but both expressed some level of dissatisfaction with the student results. In one case, the project became time-consuming without deepening the levels of content knowledge; and in the second, the teacher did not really teach students to generate creative responses. We added the thinking skills discussion to the assessment area when teaching students the steps to thinking skills, because most of the work related to the thinking skills will be students working independently (or in groups) to develop original or unique ideas and products.

Testing and Teaching Thinking

As discussed in Chapter 3, GANAG includes time for applying knowledge once the teacher has taught or given students the opportunity to learn new declarative or procedural knowledge. When we learn declarative knowledge, we should not practice or only memorize it. We learn information or vocabulary or associate facts, concepts, principles, and generalizations with what we know already, and that poses a complex thinking problem. In contrast to procedural knowledge, declarative knowledge is very easy to learn but easy to forget. We all know the feeling of remembering information for a test, only to forget most of it after a few days. More important, sometimes when we think we learn factual information, we may not really deeply understand the information or how to use it to be productive. We can answer surface-level questions but not an inferential question. Students can learn to apply declarative knowledge by using thinking skills.

When many teachers think of thinking skills, they think of Bloom's taxonomy: knowledge, comprehension, application, analysis, synthesis, and evaluation; or the updated 2018 version: remembering, understanding, applying, analyzing, evaluating, and creating. Beyond knowing and understanding, Bloom and the other assessment experts suggested that teachers apply the taxonomy to design assessments that determine "whether or not the student can remember and either cite or recognize accurate statements in response to particular questions, and also to use abstractions, display interactions, arrange patterns, use standards of appraisal [or critical evaluation], and evaluate selected or remembered materials" (1956, p. 78). In describing the taxonomy, Bloom and his colleagues wrote that testing knowledge alone constitutes only basic remembering, but the rest of the categories refer to using strategies that "emphasize the mental processes of organizing and reorganizing material to achieve a particular purpose" (p. 204).

Today, neurologists indicate that reorganizing information builds neural networks, which helps us remember more and construct new meanings. Students learn to organize and reorganize the information (taught and learned in the new information part of GANAG) in order to achieve a particular purpose. Neuroscientist Elkhonon Goldberg clearly states the particular purpose for human thinking: to generate new ideas. Writing about the prefrontal cortex in his book *The New Executive Brain: Frontal Lobes in a Complex World* (2009), Goldberg argues that you do not need frontal lobes or thinking skills to recall the idea of a girl or that of a fish. You do need frontal lobes to be able to think or to generate the idea of a mermaid. Using this example, he hypothesizes that the reason for thinking in human development, with the accompanying language that we possess, is to generate new ideas. In assessment vernacular, we refer to that as answering open-ended or inferential questions. If we want students to be able to be more proficient at constructing responses in more authentic ways, then they need to gather and organize declarative knowledge and become proficient at applying thinking skills.

In the past, Bloom's taxonomy seemed to provide a reliable structure for designing thinking tasks or assessments. Sometimes experts encourage students to go "higher" on Bloom's, but they are not sure how to provide instruction on how to do so. When asked if they have the steps for teaching the other higher-order categories of the taxonomy, most say they do not. Instead of trying to get students higher on Bloom's taxonomy or trying to attach verbs to learning goals or apps to the pyramid, we recommend explicitly teaching thinking skills with the intention of providing students with instruction and assessment for higher-order thinking using a list of thinking skills. The list of skills in Figure 4.1 draws upon a list created by Jane and her author team in *Dimensions of Learning* (Marzano et al., 1992) that they later updated with the nine high-yield strategies and newer neuroscience research on how people learn to make, retrieve, and use memory. When teaching thinking skills, teachers should provide the steps to thinking with graphic organizers that help students follow the steps to manage the content. The updated steps and discussion about teaching thinking can be found in the appendix that closes this book. You can also read more about them in *The i5 Approach: Lesson Planning That Teaches Thinking and Fosters Innovation* (Pollock & Hensley, 2018).

FIGURE 4.1
Thinking Skills

Association (identifying similarities and differences)
Compare: Describe how items are the same or different.
Classify: Group items together based on similar traits.
Make analogies: Identify a relationship or pattern between a known and an unknown situation.

Synthesis (analytical questioning)
Investigate: Explain the theme of a topic, including anything that is ambiguous or contradictory.
Construct an argument: Make a claim supported by evidence and examples.

Analysis (analytical questioning)
Analyze perspectives: Consider multiple views on an issue.
Analyze systems: Know how the parts of a system impact the whole.
Analyze reasoning for error: Recognize errors in logic.

Taking Action (generating and testing hypotheses)
Solve: Navigate obstacles to find a good solution.
Decide: Select from among seemingly equal choices.
Test: Observe, experiment, and explain.
Create: Design products or processes to meet standards and serve specific ends.

Teaching and Testing Thinking

Teaching and testing thinking are pretty straightforward if you have the tools—that is, a lesson schema that cues you to teach the thinking skills and a list of critical and creative thinking skills with the steps. Let's go back to the French

Revolution to see how Billy might use a thinking skill to design an assessment task for 10th graders.

1. Identify the standards and the content.
2. Teach the declarative knowledge and how students should take notes and organize the material.
3. Consider three or four of the thinking skills for a task, such as
   - Argument: Consider putting the king on trial, or make a claim about putting others on trial, such as the enlightened writers who generated concerns, financial leaders who supported sending military to the Americas, or the peasants who were unwilling to continue working. Choose a group, make a claim, and discuss which group was most responsible for the losses of life and prosperity.
   - Systems Analysis: Identify the decade of 1789–1799 as a system. Identify the parts and explain what would have happened differently if two or more of the parts had changed or if a different intervention had occurred. Use factual information and elaboration to hypothesize results.
   - Problem Solving: State one of the major problems with the French nation at the end of the 1700s. Offer multiple (five to seven) solutions to the problem using factual information from multiple sources. To conclude, explain the best of the solutions in detail.
4. Choose the best task or give students a choice to complete one.

In this example, the students will spend time each day taking notes: gathering and organizing the information needed to work on the thinking skills task. As the teacher lectures or provides materials, the students have shorter periods of application time each day to work on their tasks. If Billy chooses "argument," then the following steps apply:

1. Describe an event or issue.
2. Prepare and state a claim defending, refuting, or reflecting on the topic.
3. Provide detailed evidence and elaboration to defend, refute, or reflect on the topic to support the claim.
4. Offer a counterclaim with support.
5. Summarize and use the findings to generate a new perspective, caveat, or conclusion.

The N-A parts of the lesson are balanced for students to learn but also to try to reorganize the content using the steps in the thinking skill. In Billy's previous lesson, he had organized the materials and written scripts, and the students only had to spend a couple of weeks memorizing roles, not learning the historical content. Students should use thinking skills to learn a bit each day and think deeply about what they learn. Remember Goldberg's comment: the purpose of thinking is to generate new ideas. That is usually what a teacher expects when assigning projects or more comprehensive tasks that require research and presentation.

The teacher can use the steps for thinking to scaffold time-appropriate feedback to the students as they work on the projects. To communicate the findings, the teacher can suggest one or more ways for the students to present the material, by either essay or some form of multimedia presentation. In the end, students can still take a traditional test for the unit, quarter, or term.

Sarah's Science Lessons

Sarah was excited about teaching the thinking steps and said she had a chance in the next unit, when her team was going to do a science project about properties of materials. She told us, "As part of our investigation into the inquiry question, 'What is it made of and can I make it?' we were deep in the process of exploring the properties of materials, testing materials, and using our new learning to design and make things."

Properties of materials can be observed, measured, and predicted.

1. I know that objects can be described in terms of the materials they are made of (e.g., clay, cloth, paper).
2. I know about the physical properties of objects (e.g., color, size, shape, weight, texture, flexibility, attraction to magnets, floating, sinking).
3. I can measure different materials.
4. I can predict what would happen to an object depending on the material.

Sarah looked at three or four of the thinking skills, including problem solving, investigation, comparing, and classifying. She drafted a few ideas about what those tasks might look like but in the end decided on comparing. To explore the strength of materials, she said, students needed to compare materials when they tested them in order to make recommendations about whether they were strong enough to make products. The task seemed perfectly suited to comparison for students to meet the standard.

Teaching the steps to comparison would include the following:

1. Name the items to compare.
2. Tell some features about the items.
3. Say how the items are the same or different based on the features.
4. Tell what you know now (share a new idea) or could do with the information (create a new product).

Sarah told us that they began the lesson just after lunch play time while still on the playground since the students had been on the balance beams. She posed questions about the material the beams were made of and whether they could have been made of paper instead. Students discussed their thinking with a partner, many commenting to the group that paper was not heavy enough for people to stand on: "Paper is too thin and our weight is too heavy, so it would make it fall down." "When you step on it, paper would rip easily; if it is hard, it's not as easy to break." Sarah then set the learning goal for the lesson, which was posed as a question: "Is it strong?"

By watching a brief video and reading from shared materials, students learned that some materials are stronger than others, and often materials are chosen to make items based on the property of the material. They discussed different methods used to test the materials (e.g., pulling, pounding, bearing weight) and how they would decide if it was strong or not.

Students chose four materials to observe and recorded their findings on a data chart. They identified the material, something they noticed, and if they thought it was strong. They identified that some materials broke quite easily (such as tissue paper), some were harder to break (such as a plastic bag), and some did not break (such as string). At the end, they really focused on identifying the similarities and differences of the materials and responding to the question "Is it strong?"

Sarah said that in previous years when she did the activity, she thought students were thinking based on comments in the discussion. On reflection, she said she used to accept one or two examples as though everyone had answered the questions. It was by comparing four materials with each student recording findings in a chart and discussing them that this simple activity turned into an actual comparison. This was the layer that was missing from previous years: In the past, they did not have the thinking steps and the chart to collect data and analyze it. Now the discussions allowed all students to participate individually and share more higher-order comparisons.

All subject areas require students to understand some declarative knowledge, so every subject area can benefit from assessment tasks that require thinking. Teachers in our trainings often relate stories of how these tasks have deepened their students' understanding. Art teacher Adriana Rocha described the varying techniques her students used to create their ceramics projects after she introduced a comparison matrix to analyze different ceramics techniques. Elementary teacher Mike Loria told of teaching and testing the skill for forming multiple hypotheses about why different kinds of birds have differently shaped beaks. He mused, "I never thought primary students could think and articulate such details of science. In the past, they only drew the different beak adaptations and matched them to the name of the adaptation." Middle school teacher Diane Clement related how she used an analogy to scuba diving instruction to help her students understand the critical role that feedback plays in their performance, or what she calls the "life and death of learning information in 6th grade." In each case, the individual classroom teacher committed to varying the assessment tasks, testing for thinking skills, and teaching students to use the skills.

Summary

In summary, one aspect of varying assessment is deliberately teaching and testing for thinking. In the days when learning targets were discrete objectives, selected response or recall strategies worked well to identify levels of student work. Today, when our standards are more conceptual, teachers need to employ thinking skills so that the student has organized and retained information she can use to generate new insights, create original work, and springboard to new discoveries. Further, informal self-assessment and observation techniques add to the body of evidence necessary for the teacher to truly know a student's level of performance and for the student to know his or her own level of performance. That way, students can put forth the effort to learn how to improve and become responsible for their own learning.

As mentioned in Chapter 1, we explained that separating assessment tasks from grading, record keeping, and reporting would more deliberately tie instruction and assessment back to the standards, increasing feedback to students about their performances on the standards. When standards made their way into schools in the 1990s, it became evident that assessment tasks should be aligned to student progress toward meeting those standards. In this chapter we discussed assessment tasks, such as student self-assessment, standards checks, and testing thinking. In Chapter 5, we will address the curriculum standards again to explain how grading, record keeping, and reporting should align student performance to the standards for clarity and, more important, as a way to improve student progress.

Teacher Voices

McKinzie Sanders, *Science Teacher, and*
Patrick Villareal, *Math Teacher in Texas*

Atkins Middle School was *that* school, the one where teachers put in lots of extra time, but really, we were merely surviving. With a student population of roughly 85 percent low socioeconomic status, we struggled to reach our students, and our test scores proved it. While we weren't quite at the bottom of the rankings of the ten middle schools in our area, we were a far cry from the top. Our generally accepted rank was second from the bottom. Our school had overcome the status of an "unacceptable" campus, but in recent years it had become stagnant. As our principal put it, we were stuck. When testing season rolled around, we hoped for the best. We realized, however, that hope would not be enough as we faced the ever-increasing rigor of our state assessments.

In addition to the annual state assessment, our district also began administering six-week common assessments for every core content area. The district claimed, after a couple of years of evaluating the assessments, that there was a strong correlation between performance on our local tests and performance on the state test. They were right. For our school and its teachers, this meant giving our all and facing disappointing results every grading period. We knew our students were capable, but somehow we kept missing the mark. We were trying every new district incentive and strategy, but we were still not seeing the success of other schools in our area. We understood the teachers at Atkins were no different than the teachers at other campuses. If anything, we had tried more strategies to improve our teaching. What could we possibly be doing wrong?

During the first year that the two of us worked together, our principal asked for a volunteer group to begin to study a new approach to teaching and learning; we both agreed to participate. This first cohort was a group of teachers with a range of experience and content background. It was this group who began to use the Big Four approach and incorporate research-based strategies into our teaching. A year later and for subsequent years, we began to outperform other schools, once reaching second from the top, not the bottom, in school rankings!

Here is what we did.

The Science Story, by McKinzie

I was one of two science teachers in the first cohort. While I was confident that many of my own practices were beneficial to student learning, they weren't enough and I needed more.

I began by changing the purpose for the objectives I was providing to students each day. For several years previously, my school asked us to display a daily goal for students. We spent many a day in our science professional learning community discussing verbs and making sure rigor was appropriate for the standards and goals we wrote, but there was no suggestion that students had a role in setting daily objectives. Based on my school's expectations, I may have written a goal such as "Students will create a food web using pictures of animals from an aquatic ecosystem." There was such a huge emphasis placed on making sure students understood the product they were to complete that the goals became very verbose and unfriendly. Using GANAG and after a better understanding of how to set objectives, I rewrote this goal to read, "I know about the organization and relationships in a food web." This second goal implies that while students may be demonstrating their learning with the same product as before, their understanding of the product is much deeper. I was able to relay to my students that not only should they be able to create an accurate food web, they should also be able to explain the relationships within. My department began to transition from an emphasis on selecting verbs to an emphasis on expressing what we actually expected students to know by the end of the lesson.

From here, teaching students to rate themselves on their understanding at the beginning and end of class seemed like a minor adjustment. I initially had a fear that students would complete the ratings in rote compliance instead of being thoughtful about their own understanding. How I underestimated my 7th graders! It was merely a matter of time before they were not only recording ratings but were also eager to share with me their progress. My classroom transitioned into a place where students began to feel like active participants, asking me to note their progress or help when they needed it.

In order to make their goals even more meaningful, I began to look for ways to express to them exactly what a rating of 4 would look like for each class period. I would deliberately ask them to evaluate their work, and I would give specific criteria for each rating. In addition, after I had evaluated their work, I would ask them to revisit their ratings and determine how accurate they had been. Oftentimes, students were surprised to see that they had underscored themselves. I myself was surprised to see how critically they were analyzing their work and understanding.

As my learning of daily objectives developed, I learned that I could no longer write a single objective to last for days. By changing the student self-assessment, I realized why I had to change my own assessment, provide more opportunities for quizzes, and try in-class scoring. It started with a scavenger hunt to find the answers to test questions in their notebooks instead of a review; that made me realize that students wanted more quizzes and needed more feedback on a short-term basis instead of waiting to the end of a unit.

In science instruction, it was so easy to prepare a lab or project that might last for several class periods. The problem with this is that I had literally no idea what my students had accomplished until the final day. I was a deliverer of instructions and could offer no feedback until the product was complete. Sure, I answered questions along the way and helped students troubleshoot, but with 30 to a class, I had no way of knowing how each student was progressing. When I unpacked my standards into teachable pieces so that even if I intended for students to complete a project, I could measure growth each day. This meant that instead of having one goal for the entire lab, I created multiple smaller goals that students could achieve daily and that led to their understanding of the big picture. Being able to assess students on a more frequent, daily routine, I could truly monitor and adjust.

My biggest surprise was the power of the thinking skills. I remember thinking that I didn't need to teach the thinking skills because science seemed to be all about inquiry. Much to my surprise, I designed a systems analysis in which we first analyzed the school as a system and determined what would happen if specific parts changed. Then we applied the skill to the skeletal and muscular systems in a human. Just working through the steps made students more likely to participate and ask questions. They could ask about parts of the human system based on having asked and answered questions about the school. Once I realized the depth of learning and that it did not take that much more time than other activities, we did more of them. In the end, the students were much more likely to remember the science content details, and I'm sure that also contributed to better scores on our district and state assessments.

Through my work with instruction and feedback, I began to see the gains in student performances. I was thrilled to see my school climbing the rankings on district assessments like never before. Other teachers and even district personnel took notice and asked why I was experiencing such success. Since making these transitions in my classroom, 7th grade science at Atkins has maintained at least the middle ranking, if not higher, on every district assessment.

The Math Story, by Patrick

Like McKinzie, I was one out of two math teachers in the first cohort. The year we started GANAG was my very first year at Atkins. I had previously taught 6th and 7th grade math for three years in a rural school district in Texas.

I never realized how little I knew about learning until sitting through that first session about GANAG and the Big Four. Studying at the university level for two or three years, and actually teaching for three full years, I was still struggling with lesson planning and using student data to inform my teaching. My previous district did not make us turn in any lesson plans or write objectives or goals for every lesson, so in reality, my fourth year of teaching was actually my first year all over again.

I struggled that year. Dealing with a new school, new students, and lesson planning specified to goals, it was rough. After the first six-week assessment when I had 0 percent of my students meet expectations, I knew there was nowhere else to go except up.

Setting objectives was the hardest part at first. I had to study the standard and list everything the student needed to know to be successful for that standard. But as the year kept going, it became easier and I became better at setting obtainable objectives, which led to opportunities for daily student feedback. However, our district assessment data of students meeting expectations did increase every six weeks; so just by tweaking the way I taught, scores were improving in my classes.

My second year was a lot better. Teaching at a school like Atkins, the single hardest thing we face is student confidence. And let's face it, it does not matter what demographic the student belongs to; math is the subject where they have the least confidence. We really worked on the importance of the goals for the lesson and also for assessment. That was the power of the Big Four to me. Every day, the lesson to the goal was taught, and every day the students could assess themselves and I could assess them to the daily goal. In addition, we became very explicit about note taking and keeping the materials in an organized set so that the students were learning during class and had good materials to review when it came time to prepare for tests.

The students started expecting to know how they were doing, and they actually asked me for quizzes or standards checks so they would be able to track how well they really knew the material. I also began to really focus on students setting individual and class goals for their district assessments. I gave students a bar graph, and they charted what they wanted to make on the upcoming district assessment. Then when scores were in, I gave them a sticky note with the score they actually made, and they would chart that data. This connected our daily work to the progress every six weeks, and it helped.

Goals, scoring, and tracking data all made sense to me as a math guy. Critical and creative thinking were really new. I noticed that students could solve one variable of equations with variables on either side of the equal sign, but they needed to improve fluency. Using classifying, I made envelopes with about 25 equations and had them sort them, not solve them. As they sorted, they had to get fast at determining what to do, not how to do it. Groups traded envelopes, and we turned it into a task we did various times during a term. It felt like a game to them, but they got really good at the task, and that carried over to their fluency. Students like doing tasks with the thinking skills because they seem a bit different and often answer the "aha" part of math they sometimes miss when we model and do problems.

Although it took each of us as teachers to examine our own practices to see what we needed to adjust, it helped that students across the grade level had the same experiences. Since the students used the goal setting and notebooks in their other classes, they just expected it from all their teachers. Knowing they could count on tying a learning goal, instruction, and quizzes back to the content, students improved their study habits and their confidence. Our math scores increased every year the students stayed in our school, and our scores across the board in math increased as a result of our efforts.

5

Feedback and Monitoring Student Progress Aligned to the Standards

Ricky Sinfield, an elementary school teacher, was skeptical. He was wary of the new initiatives that were supposed to fix schools, test scores, even teaching, since every year there seemed to be a new framework. The Big Four seemed no different than any of the previous programs; why would it be? Other programs lasted a school year, and then the next one would be ushered in.

To stay positive but true to his own principles, Ricky developed his own strategy for the next great idea. He started asking, "Why?" He believed that asking why helped him connect the action of the task to the result. "Why will this idea improve student learning in my grade 5 class?" By asking the why question, he sometimes found out that the target or end result of the initiative for the school was not always about student learning. Schools are complex, so some initiatives would target other aspects of the broader community, such as communicating with parents, reducing paper or print material waste, and improving cultural responses. But he believed that, as a teacher, he spent most of his day focusing on students' learning, so he asked his why question about student learning.

Many teachers like Ricky, particularly experienced educators, also have doubts when it comes to the next new initiative. Indicative of this mindset are statements such as "We can wait this one out," "I wonder what new education policy will be introduced by this set of legislators," "Isn't this just like how we used to do it but with a new name?" or "That's great, but I need to get back to teaching." It doesn't help when motives behind the proposed shift may seem to be questionable, the budgets and scheduled time needed to make the change are limited or completely missing, or principles that support a successful transition and rollout are minimized or even ignored. It's no wonder a collective metaphorical (or actual) sigh can be heard when the next new idea is unveiled during the first teacher workday of the school year.

So, why the Big Four? What might be a compelling enough reason for a teacher to incorporate feedback into the tried-and-true curriculum-instruction-assessment framework that has defined our profession for decades? Chapter 1 states that the intention of curriculum-instruction-assessment was a pathway that focused on the teacher and the teaching, but the framework was missing the most important piece: a feedback loop that would directly connect student performance to the curriculum, instruction, and assessment (see Figure 5.1). That is the answer to Ricky's question: explicit feedback to the students about their progress on the standards.

Feedback to the Standards

As the reader, you know that throughout this book we specified a primary strategy for the Big Four and GANAG is providing feedback to students regularly as part of day-to-day routines. As shared in Chapter 1, setting objectives and providing feedback is one of the nine strategies that has been proven to improve achievement (Marzano et al., 2001). Confirmed again in the second edition of *Classroom Instruction That Works*, this strategy of feedback to the standards pays off significantly in student learning dividends (Dean, Ross-Hubbell, Pitler, & Stone, 2012). When students receive timely and daily feedback on how well they perform on explicitly stated goals, they will build knowledge and skills.

Remember that the Big Four weds feedback to standards that are identified as curriculum, unpacked for instruction, and monitored through assessment. This interplay between a student's understanding and performance as it relates to the standards provides direction for teachers to make instructional decisions and create opportunities for student growth and learning. So, let's take a look at how monitoring students' progress toward the standards can accomplish the goal of improving learning.

FIGURE 5.1

From Traditional Framework to the Big Four

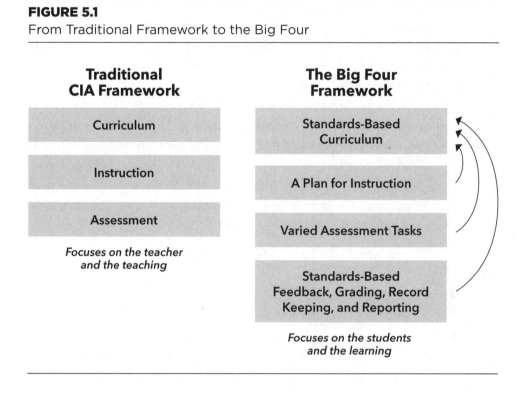

We Already Give Feedback

We are confident that you, the reader, agree with us that schools serve students as environments where "feedback is the hinge that swings the information about goals and progress between teacher and student" (Pollock, 2012, p. 5). Ricky might say to us, "We already do give feedback and already keep records on student performances." Teachers do give students verbal and written feedback and monitor their progress in grade books; this is all done in an effort to help those students perform better. Teachers tell us that they give as much feedback as they perceive to be manageable. However, there are some common complicating factors, such as the following:

- Much of teachers' verbal feedback can be categorized as directions about a task, praise, or behavior management; this type of feedback, directly addressing behavior, does not overtly guide students to improve upon curriculum standards.
- Producing written feedback is time-consuming. Given the rapid pace most teachers must maintain, it is difficult to provide written feedback within a time frame that will influence students' understanding of the

curriculum standard. The longer students wait to receive feedback on a graded assignment, the more likely they are to see the returned assignment as just a grade. Students have learned to accept grades and often are surprised when a teacher suggests that they revise and resubmit work based on written feedback.

- Most teachers' grade books are set up to track points for activities rather than by standards. Monitoring progress by activities misses the specificity of the objectives and standards that would allow for focused reteaching and differentiation.
- Many elementary and primary teachers tell us that they don't really keep grade books as much as portfolios of student work, reading records, and some assessments they use for reporting.

Most teachers recognize that giving individual feedback poses challenges, so the idea of adding more feedback and tracking student progress by the standards can be incomprehensible.

Let's take a step back for a moment and consider what we mean by feedback. It is simply information to the learner about how she is doing on a particular goal. A student needs multiple opportunities to apply knowledge (declarative) or practice skills (procedural) again and again (and sometimes again); she needs to learn to seek and receive feedback about her understanding or performance related to the daily learning objectives (standards), in order to advance or, better yet, deepen learning.

Monitoring Student Progress: Scoring to the Standards

Feedback tells a learner how he is doing; monitoring progress describes the process a teacher uses to document trends for individual student performances.

How might feedback strategies be adjusted to be more manageable and still show at least the same, if not greater, learning gains? To begin a shift in the feedback-monitoring progress paradigm for teachers, let's consider what *is* possible:

1. Most students would improve their performances on curriculum standards if they received timely feedback during class; we will call that "in-class scoring."

2. Teachers can align assignments, quizzes, and tests more explicitly to the standards so that the consistency provides accurate and useful information back to the students.

3. Teachers can score and record student performance by the objectives/standards to provide accurate feedback and use classroom data to differentiate or scaffold instruction that day or for subsequent lessons.

Based upon our work with teachers in a variety of school settings, these are strategies that, when incorporated with fidelity into a teacher's practices, improve the quality of feedback to students. In addition, the strategies can reduce teacher workload and simultaneously provide enough evidence of student learning in order to support the final grade reflected on the report card.

Before we move to explaining classroom techniques, we would like to acknowledge one issue that is real for teachers. It is important that we clarify what we mean when we use the term *monitor progress* or *progress monitoring*. Education today, particularly in the United States, is laden with accountability rules, regulations, and terminology, including efforts to ensure students do not fall between the proverbial cracks. These noble efforts are in place as a means to ensure specific educational needs are being met at the optimal times when deficits have the greatest chance of being successfully addressed, such as with dyslexia. Systems, such as the Response to Intervention approach and Multi-Tiered Systems of Support, tend to be accompanied by rigid guidelines for how progress toward goals is to be identified, measured, and documented.

In fact, talk with any educator about progress monitoring, and images of universal screening tools, numerical charts, trend lines, and cut scores are evoked. Consequently, current perceptions of progress monitoring believe that it is formulaic in nature with little flexibility, prescriptive as a result of state mandates, and detached from the daily workings within a classroom.

In the Big Four, feedback is simply timely information to students, often informal but always intentional, to make sure students know how they are progressing toward the standards taught by the teacher.

Feedback in Action

Traditionally, we think of feedback coming from one direction, usually from the teacher to the student. Instead, to richen and enhance learning, feedback should be sought by students and obtained from multiple sources: self-reflection, outside resources and research, diverse perspectives from peers, and guidance from the teacher or other specialists.

In previous chapters, we discussed the self-reflection technique where students track their own performances. During instruction and independent work, we discussed teaching students to pair/share and seek clarity about tasks from peers. Through instructional questioning, visible note taking, thinking skills, and standards checks, students will be positioned to receive feedback from the teacher. These next three strategies are routines that can be adapted into the beginning, middle, and end of lessons for students to learn about how they are doing in relation to the content and skills they are learning in class.

1. In-class scoring: Give feedback, differentiate, scaffold, and reteach during the application part of the lesson. The biggest surprise about the Big Four for Ricky Sinfield was learning to quickly assess all students right after the mini-lesson/new information. Sometimes called in-class scoring, or clipboarding, it allows teachers an informal opportunity to provide feedback to individuals and groups of students. While students work independently or in groups, teachers circulate to view student work, jotting a score for each student before pausing to help students individually. The in-class scoring data give the teacher the chance to immediately group students to reteach for differentiation. It may also serve to provide data to reorganize lessons for the next day.

Fair enough, but Ricky questioned why he needed to write the score when he would usually "keep the data in [his] head." He knew that his usual habit would have been to stop, interact with one student to reteach, and repeat with another student. He acknowledged that it did run the clock, and sometimes he retaught the same step or information to three or four students consecutively, wasting a lot of time! With in-class scoring taking about two minutes to gauge every student's progress during one walk around the classroom, he could regroup multiple students to reteach. This saved him time and ensured that he monitored progress for every student, not just the first three or four that time allowed.

Ricky's clipboard page listed student names horizontally with the standards across the top. He was surprised at the richness of the data he could collect using only a simple, 4-point scale (4 = going above, 3 = proficient, 2 = basic, and 1 = needs prompting). After a couple of days of tracking performance scores during his walkaround, Ricky realized that he needed to be more deliberate in planning instruction, especially considering differentiation in advance. After a week, he felt confident about his knowledge of the students' performance levels and was able to start using the charts to show students where they needed to practice.

Secondary teachers tend to minimize this type of observation as an assessment methodology, but they can expect it to yield the same kind of gains. For some teachers, the informality of paper-and-pencil forms on a clipboard works to collect the data. Other teachers find technology, such as computer tablets, useful because it allows them to record data electronically that can be easily referenced when conferencing with students, collaborating with co-teachers, and communicating with parents and caregivers.

In almost every classroom we watch, the teacher spends about 10 or more minutes walking around as students work independently. Since they intend to help, give feedback, and reteach immediately, this technique of in-class scoring only slightly changes their habits. Using the clipboard or device to track all students' performances capitalizes on an opportunity to reach more students with feedback and further instruction.

2. Aligning test items to the standards. Rusty Bishop, math teacher and instructional coach, uses the standards checks described in Chapter 4. He said that within the first few uses, they provided clear standards-based feedback to the students, which led to gains. As a result, he realized that the unit tests could show the items by the standards, too. That way, he and students would be able to look at the overall scores (percentages) for a general idea of performance, but they could also analyze the test results to see the areas in need of improvement. By explicitly grouping test items by standards, students would not have to retake complete tests and could focus on standards where they needed to improve. Students who showed proficiency on the standards could work on enrichment assignments or activities in order to extend their learning.

For Rusty, this technique of aligning the test items to standards improved how he used the data to help students relearn specific content. At first, he said it seemed like he was giving away information by grouping the items, but later he realized that the benefits of the reteaching and retaking was more important to students.

Rusty shared the strategy with teachers in other departments, and they were able to do the same, aligning questions to standards in order to improve retaking tests and reteaching content. This saved time, but more important, it focused follow-up teaching on areas that needed enhancement.

3. Record keeping by standards: An accurate path to the report card grade. Gary Nunnally, the social studies teacher, said he surprised himself by his changes in grading. Once students used goal sheets regularly and he started in-class scoring, he aligned his test items to the standards. Students learned ways to get help by addressing where they said they performed by standards, and Gary had his clipboard and test score evidence.

In Gary's case, he and the students were using the 1-2-3-4 scale for both goal sheets and in-class scoring. The reason was that the scale translated to 1 = not sure, 2 = know something but not enough, 3 = got it, and 4 = can go beyond. Using the 4-point scale allowed two levels below proficiency so that he and his students were able to gauge the amount of needed instruction. The goal each day would be to reach the 3.

One issue he had to address was absences. With a simple *A* in place for the absence, he could determine whether the task needed to be completed or if the subsequent tasks would fill in the gaps. He became less concerned about completion and more concerned that he was providing enough opportunities to teach and revisit the content in depth.

For a "gradeaholic," eyeballing data and using three or four test scores to generate the final grade, rather than averaging 40–50 grades for a term, was a shift. He realized, however, that all of the techniques he had incorporated were ensuring that students improved; the daily monitoring caught students when they did not understand. It would not take three or nine weeks to find that out, as it had in the past.

In a short time, Gary realized that while he wanted to put progress monitoring grades in his gradebook for assignments or classroom participation, the only grades that really counted were the quiz and test grades. The school used electronic grade books, so he submitted scores for student work regularly, but for progress reports and report cards, he found he was able to reliably use the quiz and test scores to determine the grade that would go on the report card.

Grading and Reporting to Standards

Despite numerous examples of the positive effects on student performance, standards-based grading, record keeping, and reporting continue to be somewhat controversial. Usually the reason is because schools tend to change traditional report cards to some form of standards-based reporting system before giving teachers the time and resources to successfully change their record-keeping procedures to be standards-based. In turn, there is little time to provide students and parents with details about the shift in reporting.

Feedback to the standards through instruction, in-class scoring, assignments, and quizzes is timely formative assessment and can be used as a catalyst for teachers to adjust instructional practices and better support students in improving their understanding and performance. Those data are compiled, analyzed, and summarized for reporting purposes usually two to four times a year. Summarizing does not equate to averaging, as has been the case for more than a century.

It is also important to define the following four terms in order to ensure a common understanding of assessment among students, teachers, and parents and how each is distinct yet related: feedback, grading, record keeping, and reporting. Feedback is simply information about where a student stands in relation to a goal and how to improve. Grading is the evaluation of the performance communicated by a metric or symbolic description such as 4-3-2-1, percentages, or alpha scales like *A-B-C-D-F*. Record keeping describes what teachers track in order to see trends in student growth and performances. Reporting includes scores shared in more formal ways, such as on report cards, which serve as the executive summary of an individual student's current standing.

Finally, clarifying the purposes of these four terms and the roles each play within a class helps to mitigate confusion and misunderstandings of how they may or may not affect final grades on report cards. Report cards serve as a summation of current student understanding and performance in relation to the standards. Feedback, grading, and record keeping intentionally connect the teacher and student in a flow of information intended for improvement. The flow of information, this monitoring of progress, should not negatively affect the summation for a student at "report card time," particularly when the student's understanding and performance during the early part of a unit of study were limited and just starting to develop. Likewise, early success of understanding and performance within a unit should be, at a minimum, maintained.

A school can successfully move from traditional forms of grading, such as a single percentage or letter to standards-based reporting that separates product, process, and progress criteria. Guskey (2018) states that it requires clarity in standards criteria among all stakeholders and frequent, effective communication with students and parents about how it can positively affect students' learning and future. It is important that students, parents, and caregivers understand that feedback, grading, and record keeping exist to improve student learning so as to avoid misunderstandings and surprises with the report card. Equally important, teachers can hone feedback and record-keeping practices in order to support a standards-based approach to teaching and learning. The Big Four provides the foundation needed to make it a success.

For more information about the implementation of standards-based grading, scoring, and reporting, we encourage you to consult works by educational researchers and authors such as Sue Brookhart, Thomas Guskey, Lee Ann Jung, Ken O'Connor, Tom Schimmer, and Matt Townsley.

Collaborating Teachers

Each of the strategies listed above also improves communication between co-teachers who share responsibilities for students with disabilities or temporary medical needs, students learning English, and students who may have reasons for missing school. Data gathered through in-class scoring, aligning tests back to the standards, and recording by standards are immediately usable and actionable. Small groupings of students with similar needs can seamlessly be assembled immediately, for example, after one or both of the co-teachers gather a snapshot of student understanding and performance during their walkaround in the application part of the lesson. In addition, the data can help to guide student goal setting for individualized education plans.

The Courage to Teach, the Courage to Change

It seems the *why* question posed by Ricky Sinfield would be satisfactorily answered with *what* to do to improve student learning. While for us authors it truly is about gains in student learning, it is also deeply entwined with our educational beliefs.

We believe in empowering each teacher: the practitioner within the classroom whose daily interactions help students learn. We believe in advocating for proven practices: the learning strategies that research supports. And, we believe in providing a platform for growth: sharing advancements and new discoveries for a teacher to be able to study, try out, and add to his repertoire. Our beliefs are operationalized by the Big Four:

Create a useful curriculum document that is a springboard for unit planning, weekly scheduling, and daily lesson delivery.

- Make easily accessible, user-friendly documents for the curriculum.
- Use the standards to create multiple documents for meaningful units and lessons.
- Use technology to maximize access and editing from reflection.

Use a lesson planning schema intended for master learners.

- Shift from Hunter's mastery teaching schema to Pollock's master learners schema (GANAG).
- Focus on providing opportunities for students to learn to use the nine high-yield strategies with frequent pauses for feedback.
- Organize lessons with frequent formative assessment.
- Organize sets of lessons that provide time for practice and thinking skills.

Explicitly incorporate self-assessment techniques, frequent standards checks, and thinking skills.

- Improve student engagement through self-scoring opportunities.
- Give standards checks to ensure reteaching and differentiation.
- Teach and apply thinking skills to promote real life problem solving.

Implement feedback strategies, both from the teacher and from the students, that allow for the transfer of information about progress on the standards.

- Use in-class scoring to ensure that feedback opportunities happen frequently for individuals.
- Align tests to the standards to improve reteaching and retesting opportunities.
- Simplify grading and record keeping by scoring to standards, and produce report card information that is manageable to all audiences.

We also believe each teacher—no matter who, what, or where she is teaching—can implement the Big Four successfully in her classroom regardless of whether or not the grade level, department, school, or district is adopting the Big Four. Rooted in proven strategies and evolved frameworks, we believe the Big Four are tenets of effective pedagogy. Developing a deep understanding of and fluent automaticity with the Big Four can empower a teacher to successfully change the dialogue in a classroom from being about the points and the grades to being about growth and learning.

In his book *The Courage to Teach*, Parker J. Palmer (2007) describes the courage to teach as an inward decision a teacher can make to live "divided no more." This is Palmer's way of explaining that individual teachers can and do have a positive influence on student learning when they decide not to criticize the educational institution and instead examine their own teaching practices and actions with the intent of improving student learning.

When Gary Nunnally admitted that the feedback he gave to students, kept track of in his grade book, and shared with parents was not helping students learn social studies—or study skills, for that matter—he decided to make changes. His homework policy had been a way to mask how he planned instruction. His plan book, he admitted, was not designed for student learning but for covering chapters. His tests, he alleged, required recall, not application. So, he changed. Using the Big Four and GANAG, he improved student learning and along the way, found that he loves teaching again.

Ricky Sinfield questioned every step of the way but had the courage to change. By asking why, he also found what he needed to do to adjust his teaching to improve student progress.

These teachers and so many others are brave enough to stop criticizing new initiatives and study the new information about how humans learn and the effects of teaching on learning. They are the teachers who take the time to reflect, look at their plan books and grade books, and admit that history and research clearly show us if we want all students to learn, we can do it... one teacher at a time.

Teacher Voice

Ricky Sinfield, *Elementary Teacher in London, England*

I think I was another Gary Nunnally but with primary school issues. I believe there is no silver bullet in education, no one way that outcomes can be improved for all students. Instead, I think we need to build an armory of teaching knowledge and strategies in order to improve teaching. But, even with that position, I have felt so bombarded with new and innovative strategies and knowledge that it seemed difficult to keep up; often well-intended innovations never really had a chance. So, in my teaching career, I found a way to solve the problem of too many initiatives, by simply always asking, "Why?"

Asking why has proven to be integral to my growth as a teacher. It has led to me spending my time on things that truly stand up to scrutiny and has allowed me to spend this time on innovations that can have the most impact.

You can imagine my reaction and response, then, when my principal announced to the staff that we would be adopting a new curriculum framework. A new framework that he said would affect the school up and down and would be important to every aspect of teaching and learning. Why? We are a good school with great teachers. Why do we need common vocabulary and a common instructional framework? Why not keep our individualization and autonomy as the most important way to personalize learning for students?

The principal acknowledged concerns but mostly asked the staff to trust the process. What I didn't know at the time was that the question why is one of the Big Four's strengths and what makes it stand out among a crowded field of new ideas, innovations, and practices. In fact, the framework asks the question "Why do we not see gains in student learning when teachers work so hard at their curriculum, instruction, and assessment?" The Big Four blends solid traditional teaching habits with new research-based practices, constantly reminding teachers that the goal for adjusting practices is not to improve teaching but to improve learning. If you have evidence that strategies are working for all students, keep them; but, likewise, if you have some evidence that students are not learning, then adjust that part of the framework.

The goal of the framework and the accompanying lesson planning tool was to teach so all students learn and when some do not, ask, "Why is this happening?" and "What part of my Big Four needs adjusting?"

GANAG

The GANAG lesson schema was where it all started for my colleagues and me. I listened carefully as each element of the lesson schema was explained, staying open-minded but maintaining my critical disposition—always, and I'm sure at times to everyone's frustration, asking why. Why do I need to change the way I have been planning and delivering lessons?

Goal Setting

Why do I need to teach students to set the goal for themselves? Framing a lesson with a goal was perhaps an expected start. What was unexpected, though, was the depth in the reasoning for having a lesson goal and the intricacies of having students apply the goal to themselves. If I'm honest, no one had ever taught me how to write a lesson goal before; it was a skill that you were just expected to pick up and learn. The secret, I learned, is intentionality. Being intentional when linking it back to the curriculum, being intentional when considering if it is procedural knowledge or declarative knowledge, and being intentional when assessing student progress against the curriculum. Most important was being intentional about teaching students to monitor their own progress and be able to communicate it to the teacher. Why? So students could learn to ask for more instruction when they realized they were not quite getting it.

APK

Why use time at the beginning of class to access prior knowledge? The more I researched the idea of accessing prior knowledge, the more important it seemed. Learning is not about remembering unrelated facts; it is about linking knowledge to create new and useful ideas. Starting a lesson off by piggybacking on something a student already knows is ingenious. When was the last time we learned something truly new? Everything we learn stands on the shoulders of something we already know. Why? So each student can reach into her memory and pull information forward in an intentional way that makes all the difference for remembering and also for deeply understanding new information or knowing how to shape a new skill.

New Information and Applying New Information

Why change the part of lesson planning that we do so well already? Learning new information and the application of this new knowledge are the parts of delivery that everyone thinks they are doing, myself included, until you study your lesson and realize that there is a lot of activity in lessons but not necessarily a lot of new content. Intentionality is key once again. I had never truly considered if I was teaching procedural or declarative knowledge, and as a result my teaching was the same for both. So, I'm conscious of delivering mini-lessons and following up with either practice or organizing content and apply a thinking skill. If practice, students need lots of practice, feedback, and shaping. If a thinking skill, students need to learn strategies to organize the knowledge in order to use it successfully and then work through the steps to generate original thoughts.

Goal Review

Why revisit the goal instead of just having the teacher summarize the lesson? This element is perhaps the most underrated element of lesson delivery. The reason for this is quite simply that many people do not understand why it is necessary. But, in the GANAG schema, the intentionality of the lesson goal that we see going through the whole lesson is brought to an end like the bookends of the lesson. Why? Students return to the lesson goal and rescore themselves, activating their metacognition and really considering, "Am I now a better mathematician/reader/writer than I was when I started this lesson?"

Assessment

My intention when writing about the schema above was meant less as a recap and more as a backstory to what I believe is one of the most significant but simple innovations every teacher should make: in-class scoring as a way to do progress monitoring immediately after the mini-lesson when the students begin to apply the work. It is no secret that effective and accurate assessment is key to providing feedback. Effective assessment allows us to know where our students are in relation to learning goals and thus the curriculum at any period in time. This in turn allows us to be responsive teachers, to provide immediate feedback, and to differentiate both in the moment and in the lessons to come.

In-Class Scoring

When first introduced to in-class scoring, my "why" reappeared; to say I was dubious would be an understatement. The process of scoring students in the moment as they were doing the skill was what I was already doing in my head. Why would writing it down improve student learning? But I was convinced to give it a go. Was I already doing this, or was in-class scoring about to take my teaching to the next level?

Like any new routine in teaching, this intentional type of progress monitoring took a while to truly take hold. Despite my apprehension, I noticed that something was different. As I was going down my standards and lesson goal checklist, I got to a student and almost immediately went to score him in my head and tell him to get started on the problem. Then I asked myself, "Have I actually looked properly at what this student was doing?" I had almost allowed myself to make a snap judgment about behavior; however, on closer inspection I realized that this student was struggling. As we know, with new topics come new challenges. In that moment I wrote down his real-moment score of 2 and in less than a minute checked other students. I realized that I had four students who could not actually get started, so I was able to pull them together and reteach briefly by finding out what was challenging with that task. Then, I was able to pull another three students together to give an enriched task as they finished the first. If I'm honest, I consider myself to be a very responsive teacher who knows his students well; however, it is very easy to make these assumptions, and the in-class scoring safety net had not only stopped me making a snap judgment but also ensured that I had provided the correct feedback to each student.

My next big in-class scoring moment came in a similar manner, but this time as I looked down the list, I got to a student who was not struggling and was not excelling in this topic. Normally I wouldn't have thought twice about allowing that student to continue cruising through the work. However, on this occasion I gave a true score and then used that score to challenge him to take his work to the next level. I looked at my score sheet and used it to remind this student what the lesson goal was and the knowledge I was asking him to apply, aided by the curriculum objective. I challenged him not to cruise but to take his writing to the next level. And he did. Without going through the process of writing down each student's score, I honestly believe that I would have nonchalantly skipped over that student. But the formal process of in-class scoring had stopped me from doing this and had ensured my feedback was linked back to both the lesson goal and the curriculum standard.

Conclusion

As teachers, we have a huge responsibility. We are tasked with educating the future citizens of the world. In a classroom we make thousands of in-the-moment decisions that affect each and every student. People around us try relentlessly to help us with this monumental task; however, more often than not, this help is also relentless and overwhelming.

What if every time someone offered us advice or implemented a new innovation, we asked, "Why do this? Will this improve student learning for some students?" This is the litmus test for improving my teaching and student learning. Why should I use or implement the Big Four? If I'm honest, I expected it to fail. A year later, our principal celebrated our test scores; yes, we actually did a schoolwide dance in a large assembly—you might know how to do it: "the floss." We are a dedicated staff, and we trusted the process that resulted in our school showing overwhelming gains across literacy and math in one year. There were no other initiatives, no changes in student enrollments, no other reasons for the extraordinary gains other than teachers reflecting on their own practices and applying the research on learning to slightly adjust some classroom practices. And a couple of years later, we were able to sustain the gains.

I can honestly say that this has made me a better teacher and made it easier for me to communicate with colleagues because we share a common vocabulary based on research. Now be honest with me: how many initiatives have you implemented that have truly made you a better teacher? Maybe a few, you say. But how many have you implemented that have not only made you a better teacher but have also made your students better learners? That, I say, is the difference the Big Four can make, and that is where true improvement can be found.

Acknowledgments

Many thanks to you, the teachers who invited us into your classrooms, shared lessons over Skype, and trusted the process. Your dedication to improve learning for all students by enhancing your own practice is inspiring.

Megan Doyle, editor, and Genny Ostertag, acquisitions director, thanks for your encouragement and guidance. We appreciate you and all of the ASCD staff who contributed to the publication process.

Appendix:
Thinking Skills Processes

Association

Compare: Describe how items are the same or different.

1. Identify the items to compare. (Comparing three or more items makes the comparison more ambiguous and, therefore, more complex.)
2. Identify features by which to associate the items.
3. State how the items are similar or different based on the features.
4. Summarize findings to generate new ideas or insights.

Simplified Language

1. Name the items to compare.
2. Tell some features about the items.
3. Say how the items are the same or different based on the features.
4. Tell what you know now (share a new idea) or could do with the information (create a new product).

Classify: Group items together based on shared traits.

1. Identify multiple items to sort.
2. Sort the items based on a single or multiple attributes.
3. Reorganize or regroup items.
4. Summarize findings to generate new ideas or products.

Simplified Language

1. Name items to classify.
2. Sort the items and say why they are in a group.

3. Say how items could go into different groups.
4. Tell what you know now (share a new idea) or could do with the information (create a new product).

Create Analogies: Identify a relationship or pattern between a known and an unknown situation.

1. Identify an event or topic that is difficult to understand.
2. Identify a familiar situation describing the steps or the parts in general terms.
3. Explain the new event or topic using the familiar situation to guide the narrative.
4. Summarize understandings and generate insights about the new event or topic.

Simplified Language

1. Tell about a topic that is hard to understand.
2. Explain a familiar story or experience in your own words.
3. Tell how each part of what you know works, so you can explain the new topic.
4. Tell what you know now (share a new idea) or could do with the information (create a new product).

Synthesis

Investigate: Explain the theme of a topic, including anything that is ambiguous or contradictory.

1. Identify a topic to study or research.
2. State the ambiguity or contradiction about the topic and gather information.
3. Clarify the ambiguous or contradictory issues to extract the theme and gather more information, if necessary.
4. Summarize understandings and generate insights about the topic.

Simplified Language

1. Describe something or something that happened.
2. Say the main idea about the topic, or what is unique or unusual about it.
3. Read and gather information to explain the confusion.
4. Tell what you know now (share a new idea) or could do with the information (create a new product).

Argue: Make a claim supported by evidence and examples.

1. Describe an event or issue.
2. Prepare and state a claim defending, refuting, or reflecting on the topic.
3. Provide detailed evidence and elaboration about the claim.
4. Offer a counterclaim with support.
5. Summarize and use the findings to generate a new insight about the event or issue.

Simplified Language

1. Tell about a situation.
2. State your opinion about the situation.
3. Explain your opinion with examples.
4. State an opposite opinion about the situation.
5. Tell what you know now or how to make the situation better.

Analysis

Analyze Perspectives: Consider multiple takes on an issue.

1. Describe an event or issue.
2. State a viewpoint that is expressed, supported by logic and evidence.
3. Explain other viewpoints expressed, referencing supporting logic and evidence.
4. Explain the strengths, weaknesses, and unique features of the different viewpoints.
5. Summarize and use the findings to generate a new insight about the event or issue.

Simplified Language

1. Describe a situation.
2. Tell how one person sees it.
3. Tell how a different person sees it.
4. Give your opinion about the differences.
5. Explain what you know now or how to make it better.

Analyze Systems: Know how the parts of a system impact the whole.

1. Identify an object, event, or thing as a system.
2. Describe its parts and how they function.
3. Change a part or function and explain how it affects the whole.

4. Change another part and explain the results. (This step can be repeated multiple times.)

5. Summarize and use the findings to generate deeper understanding or an improvement to the system.

Simplified Language

1. Name something you will think about as a system.
2. Tell how the parts of it work.
3. Change one part and tell how the whole thing works now.
4. Do it again with a different part.
5. Explain what you know now about the thing or how to make it better.

Analyze Reasoning for Error: Recognize errors in thinking.

1. Describe an event, situation, or argument that is presented to you.
2. Identify the tactics (fallacies) used to manipulate the truth.
3. Explain possible misunderstandings based on the error in reasoning.
4. Summarize and use findings to generate a new idea or product.

Simplified Language

1. Tell about a situation or opinion.
2. Say what the presenter is trying to get you to believe.
3. Explain what might not be true.
4. Explain what you believe to be true.

Taking Action

Solve: Navigate obstacles to find a good solution to a problem.

1. Describe a situation that involves a goal.
2. Explain a barrier or barriers that prevent accomplishing the goal.
3. Identify multiple solutions to meet the goal.
4. Try a solution to overcome the barrier.
5. Repeat with other solutions.
6. Explain which solution you will use and how you will take action.

Simplified Language

1. Identify a goal.
2. Explain something that gets in the way of reaching the goal.
3. Identify a few ways to solve the problem.
4. Try one of the ways to see how it works.

5. Try another way.
6. Use what you learned to take action.

Decide: Select from among seemingly equal choices.

1. Describe a situation and the decision you want to make.
2. List the different alternatives you want to consider.
3. State various criteria that are important to consider and assign an importance score (e.g., 1–4).
4. Rate each alternative on a scale (e.g., 1–4) to show the extent to which each alternative meets each criterion.
5. For each alternative, multiply the importance score and the rating and then add the products to indicate a score for each alternative.
6. Determine which alternative has the highest score and use it as your choice or to determine how you will take action.

Simplified Language

1. Describe a decision you want to make.
2. List your choices.
3. List the features that are important to you to make the choice.
4. Give a number of tokens or marks to each feature to show its value.
5. For each choice, now place those tokens or marks to show importance.
6. Identify the choice with the highest number of tokens or marks and tell how you will take action.

Test: Observe, experiment, and explain.

1. Observe an event or situation.
2. Explain what you observe and might infer.
3. Make a prediction or state a hypothesis.
4. Create a test or survey to test your prediction.
5. Collect data and organize the results.
6. Draw a conclusion and use findings to describe how to take action.

Simplified Language

1. Observe an event or situation.
2. Explain what you see or understand to be happening.
3. Predict something that can be tested.
4. Set up a test or survey.
5. Collect data and organize the results.
6. Use what you learned to take action.

Create: Design products or processes to meet standards and serve specific ends.

1. Describe a need to meet or a desired end.
2. Determine a set of standards for success.
3. Design a prototype or a draft.
4. Seek feedback to improve on the idea or product.
5. Edit or revise until the need appears to be met.
6. Take action to produce, publish, or share the innovation.

Simplified Language

1. Think of something that needs to exist or be better.
2. Explain what it should look like or be like.
3. Make a model.
4. Listen to what others have to say about how to make it better.
5. Make it better.
6. Produce, publish, or share it.

References and Resources

Bloom, B. (Ed.). (1956). *Taxonomy of educational objectives*. New York: David McKay.

Brown, P. C., Roediger, H. L., & McDaniel, M. A. (2014). *Make it stick: The science of successful learning*. Cambridge, MA: Harvard University Press.

Common Core State Standards Initiative. (2010a). *Common Core State Standards for English language arts*. Washington, DC: National Governors Association and CCSSO. Retrieved from http://www.corestandards.org/ELA-Literacy/

Common Core State Standards Initiative. (2010b). *Common Core State Standards for mathematics*. Washington, DC: National Governors Association and CCSSO. Retrieved from http://www.corestandards.org/Math

Cooney, W., Cross, C., & Trunk, B. (1993). *From Plato to Piaget*. Lanham, MD: University Press of America.

Dean, C. B., Ross-Hubbell, E., Pitler, H., & Stone, B. (2012). *Classroom instruction that works: Research-based strategies for increasing student achievement* (2nd ed.). Alexandria, VA: ASCD.

Duke, N. K., & Pearson, P. (2002). Effective practices for developing reading comprehension. In A. E. Farstrup & S. J. Samuels (Eds.), *What research has to say about reading instruction* (3rd ed., pp. 205–242). Newark, DE: International Reading Association.

English, F. W. (1986, December–1987, January). It's time to abolish conventional curriculum guides. *Educational Leadership, 37*, 50–52. Retrieved from http://www.ascd.org/ASCD/pdf/journals/ed_lead/el_198612_english.pdf

Gagne, R. M. (1965). *The conditions of learning*. New York: Holt, Rinehart and Winston.

Glass, G. V., & Hopkins, K. D. (1984). *Statistical methods in education and psychology*. Upper Saddle River, NJ: Prentice Hall.

Goldberg, E. (2009). *The new executive brain: Frontal lobes in a complex world*. New York: Oxford University Press.

Goodlad, J. I. (1984). *A place called school*. New York: McGraw-Hill.

Guskey, T. R. (2018, February 4). Multiple grades: The first step to improving grading and reporting. *Education Week*. Retrieved from https://blogs.edweek.org/edweek/

leadership_360/2018/02/multiple_grades_the_first_step_to_improving_grading_and_reporting.html

Hattie, J. (2009). *Visible learning: A synthesis of over 800 meta-analyses relating to achievement.* New York: Routledge.

Hunter, M. (1982). *Mastery teaching.* Thousand Oaks, CA: Corwin Press.

Mager, R. (1962). *Preparing objectives for programmed instruction.* Atlanta, GA: CEP Press.

Marzano, R. J., Pickering, D. J., Arredondo, D. E., Blackburn, G. J., Brandt, R. S., Moffett, C. S., & Pollock, J. E. (1992). *Dimensions of learning teacher's manual.* Alexandria, VA: ASCD.

Marzano, R. J., Pickering, D. J., & Pollock, J. E. (2001). *Classroom instruction that works.* Alexandria, VA: ASCD.

New York State Education Department. (2016). *Curriculum and instruction.* Albany: Author. Retrieved from www.nysed.gov/curriculum-instruction

Ornstein, A., Levine, D., & Gutek, G. (1993). *Foundations of education* (5th ed.). Boston: Houghton Mifflin.

Palmer, P. (2007). *The courage to teach.* 10th Anniversary Edition. San Francisco: Jossey-Bass.

Pearson, P. D., & Gallagher, G. (1983, July). The instruction on reading comprehension. *Contemporary Educational Psychology, 8*(17), 317–344.

Pollock, J. E. (2012). *Feedback: The hinge that joins teaching and learning.* Thousand Oaks, CA: Corwin.

Pollock, J. E., & Hensley, S. (2018). *The i5 approach: Lesson planning that teaches thinking and fosters innovation.* Alexandria, VA: ASCD.

Rothstein, R. (1998). *The way we were? The myths and realities of America's student achievement.* New York: Century Foundation Press.

Schimmer, T., Hillman, G., & Stalets, M. (2018). *Standards-based learning in action: Moving from theory to practice.* Bloomington, IN: Solution Tree.

Snyder, T. (Ed.). (1993). *120 years of American education: A statistical portrait.* Washington, DC: National Center for Education Statistics. Retrieved from http://nces.ed.gov/pubs93/93442.pdf

Stigler, J. W., & Hiebert, J. (1999). *The teaching gap.* New York: Free Press.

Stigler, J. W., & Stevenson, H. W. (1992). *The learning gap.* New York: Summit Books.

Tennessee Department of Education. (2016). *Academic standards.* Nashville: Author. Retrieved from www.tn.gov/education/instruction/academic-standards.html

Tyler, R. (1949). *Basic principles of curriculum and instruction.* Chicago: University of Chicago Press.

U.S. Department of Education National Committee on Excellence in Education. (1983). *A nation at risk: The imperative for educational reform.* Washington, DC: Author. Retrieved from www.ed.gov/pubs/NatAtRisk/index.html

U.S. Department of Labor Secretary's Commission on Achieving Necessary Skills. (1991, June). *What work requires of schools: A SCANS report for America.*

Washington, DC: Author. Retrieved from http://wdr.doleta.gov/SCANS/what-work/whatwork.pdf

Online Resources

Arkansas Academic Standards: http://dese.ade.arkansas.gov/divisions/learning-services/curriculum-and-instruction

History of CTE: https://www.acteonline.org/wp-content/uploads/2018/02/Independent-Action_1826-1876.pdf

Missouri Learning Standards: https://dese.mo.gov/college-career-readiness/curriculum/missouri-learning-standards

National Center for Education Statistics Publications Search Page: http://nces.ed.gov/pubsearch

National Council of Teachers of Mathematics (NCTM): http://nctm.org

New York Standards: http://www.nysed.gov/curriculum-instruction

Next Generation Science Standards: https://www.nextgenscience.org/standards/standards

No Child Left Behind: www.ed.gov/nclb/landing.jhtml

Tennessee Department of Education Academic Standards: www.tn.gov/education/instruction/academic-standards.html

Index

The letter *f* following a page locator denotes a figure.

absences, grading, 108
    access prior knowledge (APK), 61,
      63–65, 77–78, 113–114
acquire new information, 65–67, 78, 114
acquire new skills, 65–66
analysis, thinking skills process, 91*f*,
  119–120
apply knowledge, 67–68, 78–79
assessment
    beneficiaries of, 80
    Big Four framework, 5
    end-of-schooling, 10–11
    formative, 81–82, 86
    goals/objectives, scoring, 60, 61*f*, 62*f*,
      82–85
    historically, 8–10
    learning and, 80–81
    perceptions of, 80
    recommendations to improve results,
     81
    self-assessment by students, 68–69,
     82–85, 110
    of standards, 4
    standards-based, 107
    summative, 81–82, 95
    teacher voice on, 96–100, 114
    thinking skills, 87–95

assessment terminology, 108–109
assessment tools
    electronic goal sheets, 85
    goal sheets, 83–84
    notebook headers, 84–85
    quizzes, 85–87
    standards checks for content, 85–87
association, thinking skills process, 91*f*,
  117–118

*The Basic Principles of Curriculum and
  Instruction* (Tyler), 8
basketball, 21–22
behavioral objectives, 9, 43
benchmarks, 11
Big Four framework
    author beliefs regarding the, 110–111
    conclusion, teacher voice, 116
    focus of, 13–14
    foundational elements, 6–8
    implementing the, 111
    resistance to the, 101–102
    summary, 15
    traditional model compared, 5–6, 6*f*,
     103*f*
Big Four framework, teacher voice on
    basketball compared, 21–22

Big Four framework, teacher voice on—
(*continued*)
  collaboration, collegial, 17–18
  conclusions, 116
  from points to performance, 17–20
  GANAG schema strategies, 112–116
  grades, moving away from, 19–21
  high-performing students, 25
  listening and learning, 17
  low-performing students, 23–24
  new challenges, meeting, 20–21
  parent–teacher meetings, 22–23
  reasons for using, 116
  teaming with the special education
    department, 24
Bill for the More General Diffusion of
  Knowledge, 11

Classroom Instruction That Works
  (Marzano et al.), 57, 102
classrooms, present-day, 12
clipboarding, 106–107
collaboration, collegial, 17–18, 109–110
content, acquiring new, 65–66
The Courage to Teach (Palmer), 111
course descriptions, writing and reviewing, 33–34
curriculum
  Big Four framework, 5
  useful, 28–29
curriculum design, 25
curriculum development, 9, 44–47
curriculum documents
  course description in, 33–34
  declarative and procedural knowledge
    statements, 42–43, 43*f*
  deleting process, 33
  standards connecting, 32–33
  unfriendly formats, 3–4
  useful, 26–29, 110
curriculum documents organization
  desired, 29, 30*f*

curriculum documents organization—
(*continued*)
  lesson goals, 40–42
  overall course document, 30, 31, 32*f*,
    33–34
  standards, grouping by, 37
  standards distributed reporting
    period, 37
  standards pacing matrix, 35–37, 35*f*,
    36*f*
  technology in revising, 29–30
  traditional, 29
  unit plans, 37–38, 39*f*, 40
  year/semester past units, 34–35, 34*f*
curriculum housekeeping, 44–46, 45*f*
curriculum initiatives, 28
curriculum-instruction-assessment
  model, 3–6, 3*f*, 6*f*, 9–10
curriculum objectives, historically, 8–10

Dimensions of Learning (Marzano et al.),
  91

education
  historically, 7–8
  outcome-based, 10–11
effective schools movement, 10
Elementary and Secondary Education
  Act, 11
Every Student Succeeds Act, 11

feedback
  Big Four framework, 5
  in the GANAG schema, 69
  improving, strategies for, 104–105
  meaning of, 108
  to motivate, 19–20
  standards-based, 5, 102, 107
  typical, complicating factors in,
    103–104
  verbal, 103
  written, 103–104

feedback strategies
    align test items to standards, 107
    in-class scoring, 106–107
    implementing, 110–111
    record-keeping by standards, 107–108
football skills, 87–88

GANAG schema
    extending the lesson with homework,
      69
    feedback in the, 69
    introduction, 14–15
    lesson planning within the, 70, 71*f*,
      72–73*f*
    strategies overview, 58–59
    technology and, 70
    transformation to, 14–15
GANAG schema strategies
    access prior knowledge (APK), 61,
      63–65, 77–78, 113–114
    acquire new information, 65–67, 78,
      114
    apply knowledge, 67–68, 78–79, 114
    goal review, 68–69, 79, 114
    goals/objectives, writing and scoring,
      60, 61*f*, 62*f*, 77
    teacher voice on, 112–116
goals
    for lessons, 40–42
    monitoring progress toward, 104–105
    reviewing, 68–69, 79, 114
    setting, 113
goal sheets, 83–85
goals/objectives, writing and scoring, 60,
    61*f*, 62*f*, 77, 82–85, 113, 115
grades/grading
    absences, 108
    accurate, 107–108
    meaning of, 108–109
    moving away from, 19–21, 107–108
    report cards, 107–108, 109
    standards-based, 108, 109

graduation rates, 12–13

homework, 1, 17, 69
hope, replacing with certainty, 2

*i5 Approach: Lesson Planning That
    Teaches Thinking and Fosters Innova-
    tion* (Pollock & Hensley), 91
in-class scoring, 106–107, 115
Individuals with Disabilities Education
    Act (IDEA), 12
information, acquiring new, 65–67, 78,
    114
instruction events, 54–55

know, understand, and do (KUD)
    method, 41
knowledge
    access prior (APK), 61, 63–65, 77–78,
      113–114
    applying, 67–68, 78–79, 114
    declarative and procedural, 42–43,
      44*f*, 57, 65–68, 89–90
    high-yield strategies to retain, 57–58

learning
    feedback and, 102
    knowledge about, 57
    testing and, 80–81
The Learning Gap (Stigler & Stevenson),
    13
learning goal ladders, 42
learning objectives, 40
learning strategies, 57–58, 85–87
lesson planning
    attaching standards with, 3–4
    collaborative, 17–18
    daily, 52–53
    declarative and procedural knowledge
      in, 42–43, 44*f*
    historically, 54
    instruction events model, 54–55

lesson planning—(*continued*)
   lesson goals, just-right, 40–42
   for master learners, 110
   summary, 74–75
   teacher remembrances, 51–52
   workshop model, 55
lessons, wraparound, 56

Make It Stick: The Science of Successful Learning (Brown, Roediger, & McDaniel), 80
master learners, 57–59, 110
mastery teaching, 53, 56, 58, 110
Mastery Teaching (Hunter), 53, 56, 58
motivation, feedback for, 19–20

A Nation at Risk (DOE), 10
The New Executive Brain: Frontal Lobes in a Complex World (Goldberg), 90
No Child Left Behind (NCLB), 11, 12
notebook headers, 84–85
notebooks, interactive, 66–67
note taking, 66

Old Deluder Satan Act, 7
120 Years of American Education: A Statistical Portrait (Snyder), 12
outcome-based education, 10–11

pacing matrix, 35–37, 35*f*, 36*f*
parent–teacher meetings, 22–23
pedagogical automaticity, 13, 53, 56, 58, 70, 74
A Place Called School (Goodlad), 12
points, moving away from, 17–20
professional development, resisting, 16
progress monitoring, 104–105

question why, 112–113
quizzes, 85–87

Race to the Top initiative, 11
record keeping
   meaning of, 109
   standards-based, 107–108
report cards, 107–108, 109
reporting
   meaning of, 109
   standards-based, 108–109

self-assessment by students, 68–69, 82–85, 110
sketchnoting, 67
skills acquisition, 65–66
special education department, 24
standards
   21st century, 87
   aligning test items to the, 107
   background, 8–11
   in curriculum documents, 32–33
   feedback to the, 101–102
   formatting for usefulness, 32–33
   grading and reporting to, 108–109
   grouping by reporting period, 37
   I do/I know statements, 40–41
   record keeping by, 107–108
   scoring progress to the, 104–105
   term usage, 32
   unpacking, 40
Standards-Based Learning in Action: Moving from Theory to Practice (Schimmer, Hillman, & Stalets), 41
standards distribution matrix, 35–37, 35*f*, 36*f*
standards movement, 11
students
   high-performing, 25
   low-performing, 23–24
   present-day, 12–13
   self-assessment by, 68–69, 82–85, 110
synthesis, thinking skills process, 91*f*, 118–119

taking action, thinking skills process, 91*f*, 120–122

Taxonomy of Educational Objectives (Bloom, ed.), 8

teachers
empowering, 110
present-day, 13–14

teacher voice
assessment, 96–100
Big Four framework, 16–25, 116
curriculum leader, 48–50

teacher voice, GANAG schema strategies
access prior knowledge (APK), 77–78, 113–114
acquire new information, 78, 114
apply knowledge, 78–79, 114
assessment, 114
goal review, 79, 114
goals/objectives, writing and scoring, 77, 113, 115
looking ahead, 79
the question why, 112–113

teaching, learning, 13, 53

The Teaching Gap (Stigler & Hiebert), 13

technology
electronic goal sheets, 85
GANAG schema and, 70

thinking, purpose of, 90

thinking skills
categories of, 67
for higher-order thinking, 91*f*
planning for, 67–68
testing, 87–95

thinking skills processes
analysis, 91*f*, 119–120
association, 91*f*, 117–118
synthesis, 91*f*, 118–119
taking action, 91*f*, 120–122

time, available, 19

unit plans
distributing standards into, 37–38, 40
sample, 39*f*
translating into action, 40

Visible Learning (Hattie), 83

What Work Requires of Schools, SCANS-Report on Workplace Skills (DOL), 10

workplace requirements, 10

workshop model, 55

About the Authors

Jane E. Pollock, PhD, coauthor of the ASCD bestseller *Classroom Instruction That Works* (2001), works worldwide with teachers, coaches, and principals on instruction and supervision. Her work results in improved student achievement at the classroom and school levels.

Jane worked as a teacher, district administrator, and senior researcher at McREL Research Laboratory. Jane wrote *Improving Student Learning One Teacher at a Time* (2007) and *Feedback: The Hinge That Joins Teaching and Learning* (2012). She coauthored *Dimensions of Learning Teacher's Manual* (1997) and *Dimensions of Learning Training Manual* (1996), *Assessment, Grading and Record Keeping* (1999), *Classroom Instruction That Works* (2001), *Improving Student Learning One Principal at a Time* (2009), *Minding the Achievement Gap One Classroom at a Time* (2012), and *The i5 Approach: Lesson Planning That Teaches Thinking and Fosters Innovation* (2018).

Jane attained degrees at the University of Colorado at Boulder and Duke University.

Laura J. Tolone has served students for the past 25 years in U.S. and worldwide school communities as a teacher, an athletic coach, a librarian, an administrative leader, and a consultant. She specializes in building student-centered cultures that improve learning. Laura spent the past 15 years in the Dominican Republic working with teachers to incorporate standards-based strategies into daily practices of teaching and learning. Her conviction for doing what is best for students drives the work she continues to do every day with fellow educators.

A native of Normal, Illinois, Laura earned degrees at Millikin University (Decatur, Illinois) and Dominican University (River Forest, Illinois). Her post-graduate work paved pathways for her to obtain an administrative credential from DePaul University (Chicago, Illinois), and she became a Fellow of the Association for Advancement of International Education (AAIE) by completing an international school leadership program from Wilkes University (Wilkes-Barre, Pennsylvania).

Related ASCD Resources

At the time of publication, the following resources were available (ASCD stock numbers in parentheses).

Print Products

Ditch the Daily Lesson Plan: How do I plan for meaningful student learning? (ASCD Arias) by Michael Fisher (#SF116036)

Ensuring High-Quality Curriculum: How to Design, Revise, or Adopt Curriculum Aligned to Student Success by Angela Di Michele Lalor (#116006)

The i5 Approach: Lesson Planning That Teaches Thinking and Fosters Innovation by Jane E. Pollock with Susan Hensley (#117030)

Improving Student Learning One Principal at a Time by Jane E. Pollock and Sharon M. Ford (#109006)

High-Quality Lesson Planning (Quick Reference Guide) by Jane E. Pollock, Susan Hensley, and Laura Tolone (#QRG118050)

Minding the Achievement Gap One Classroom at a Time by Jane E. Pollock, Sharon M. Ford, and Margaret M. Black (#112005)

Solving 25 Problems in Unit Design: How do I refine my units to enhance student learning? (ASCD Arias) by Jay McTighe and Grant Wiggins (#SF115046)

Upgrade Your Curriculum: Practical Ways to Transform Units and Engage Students by Janet A. Hale and Michael Fisher (#112014)

For up-to-date information about ASCD resources, go to **www.ascd.org**. You can search the complete archives of *Educational Leadership* at **www.ascd .org/el**.

ASCD myTeachSource®

Download resources from a professional learning platform with hundreds of research-based best practices and tools for your classroom at http:// myteachsource.ascd.org

For more information, send an e-mail to member@ascd.org; call 1-800-933-2723 or 703-578-9600; send a fax to 703-575-5400; or write to Information Services, ASCD, 1703 N. Beauregard St., Alexandria, VA 22311-1714 USA.

WHOLE CHILD
TENETS

1 HEALTHY

Each student enters school healthy and learns about and practices a healthy lifestyle.

2 SAFE

Each student learns in an environment that is physically and emotionally safe for students and adults.

3 ENGAGED

Each student is actively engaged in learning and is connected to the school and broader community.

4 SUPPORTED

Each student has access to personalized learning and is supported by qualified, caring adults.

5 CHALLENGED

Each student is challenged academically and prepared for success in college or further study and for employment and participation in a global environment.

THE WHOLE CHILD

The ASCD Whole Child approach is an effort to transition from a focus on narrowly defined academic achievement to one that promotes the long-term development and success of all children. Through this approach, ASCD supports educators, families, community members, and policymakers as they move from a vision about educating the whole child to sustainable, collaborative actions.

Improving Students One Teacher at a Time, 2nd Edition relates to the **engaged** and **supported** tenets. *For more about the ASCD Whole Child approach, visit* **www.ascd.org/wholechild.**